potential  difference

presents

T0347053

DARKNET

ROSE LEWENSTEIN

Darknet was first performed at
Southwark Playhouse, London, on 14 April 2016

DARKNET

ROSE LEWENSTEIN

CAST

Jamie	**Jim English**
Steve/Mitch/ensemble	**Robin Berry**
Stacey/Charlotte/ensemble	**Rosie Thomson**
Gary/John/ensemble	**Naveed Khan**
Allen	**Gyuri Sarossy**
Kyla	**Ella McLoughlin**
Candy/Rachel/ensemble	**Greer Dale-Foulkes**

CREATIVE TEAM

Director	**Russell Bender**
Designer	**Mila Sanders**
Lighting Designer	**Katharine Williams**
Sound Designer	**Edward Lewis**
Video Designer	**Benjamin Walden**
Movement Directors	**Jennifer Jackson**
	Russell Bender
Creative Technologist	**Henry Garner**
Creative Associates	**William Drew**
	Wendy Kibble
Dialect Coach	**Luke Nicholson**
Associate Producer	**Kendall Masson**
Production Manager	**Ed Borgnis**
Company Stage Manager	**Benjamin Luke**
Design Assistant	**Alice Simonato**
Assistant Lighting Designer	**Sana Yamaguchi**
Marketing Consultants	**JHI Marketing**
Press	**Kate Morley PR**
	(www.katemorleypr.com)

Darknet is the third collaboration between Rose Lewenstein and Russell Bender. Their process usually starts with a big idea. Rose always writes, Russell always directs, but they work closely together from the outset, with each phase of research, writing and development informing the next.

CAST

ROBIN BERRY (Steve/Mitch/ensemble)
Theatre credits include *Dagestan* (Penned in the Margins); *The Elephant Man* (South East Asia tour); *One Man, Two Guvnors* (National Theatre). Film and television credits include *Jungle Book: Origins, Urban Hymn, Arthur & Merlin, Clash of the Titans, Descent 2, Silent Witness* and *Law & Order UK*.

GREER DALE-FOULKES (Candy/Rachel/ensemble)
Theatre credits include *The Playboy of the Western World* (Southwark Playhouse); *The Provoked Wife* (GoPeople); *Gibraltar* (Arcola Studio); *The Tempest* (Watermill, Newbury); *While the Sun Shines* (Lion & Unicorn); *This Year It Will Be Different* (Theatre503); *Head/Heart* (Box of Tricks tour/Theatre503); *Lidless* (Trafalgar Studios/HighTide); *One Night in November* (Coventry Belgrade); *The Theatre Ep* (HighTide/Latitude); *Lulu* (Gate); *Judgement Day* (Almeida). Television credits include *Call the Midwife, Holby City, The Last Station*; and for film, *Magpie*.

JIM ENGLISH (Jamie)
Jim grew up in Hull and trained at Rose Bruford. Theatre credits include *Dancing Through the Shadows* (Hull Truck); *Hurling Rubble at the Moon* (Park); *Death at Dawn* (Cloud Nine/Linskill Centre); *Solid Air* (Theatre Royal Plymouth); *What You Will* (Shakespeare's Globe); *Harvest* (Greenwich); *Happy Hour* (Hull Truck/Bench Marks). Television credits include *New Blood*; *Doctors*; and for film, *The Pact* and *Gone*.

NAVEED KHAN (Gary/John/ensemble)
Theatre credits include *Pitcairn* (Shakespeare's Globe/Out of Joint/CFT); *Pioneer, After the Rainfall* (Curious Directive); *59 Minutes to Save Christmas* (Sheffield Theatres/Barbican/Slung Low); *The Trial* (Watford Palace Theatre); *The Truth Teller* (King's Head); *Lincoln Road* (Eastern Angles). Television credits include *Birds of a Feather, Catherine Tate's Nan* and *River*. Film credits include *Survivor* and *Second Coming*.

ELLA McLOUGHLIN (Kyla)
Ella trained at LAMDA and recently made her professional stage debut in *Herons* (Lyric Hammersmith).

GYURI SAROSSY (Allen)
Theatre credits include *Creditors* (Young Vic); *The Absence of War, The Seagull, Earthquakes in London* (Headlong); *The Widowing of Mrs Holroyd* (Orange Tree); *Tonight at 8.30* (English Touring Theatre); *'Tis Pity She's a Whore* (Cheek by Jowl); *Foxfinder* (Finborough); *As You Like It* (Manchester Royal Exchange); *The Seven Year Itch* (Salisbury Playhouse); *The Ragged Trousered Philanthropists* (Liverpool Everyman/Chichester Festival); *Romeo and Juliet* (RSC); *Luther* (National Theatre); *Man and Superman, Don Juan,*

Galileo's Daughter (Peter Hall Company); *The Hypochondriac* (Almeida); *Uncle Vanya, Twelfth Night* (Donmar Warehouse); title roles in *Coriolanus* and *Macbeth* (Shakespeare at the Tobacco Factory) and *The Promise* (Tricycle). Film credits include *Mercenaries, Another Life* and *Until Death.* Television credits include *The Coroner, Foyle's War, Einstein and Eddington, Tchaikovsky, Egypt* and *Judge John Deed.*

ROSIE THOMSON (Stacey/Charlotte/ensemble)
Theatre credits include *Stinkfoot, The Manual Oracle* (The Yard); *Starlore for Beginners* (Theatre503); *Fracture/Two Fish* (HighTide); *Stepping Out* (Salisbury Playhouse); *Don Juan Comes Back From the War* (Finborough); *The Kitchen, The Cherry Orchard* (National Theatre); *Fen* (Finborough/NT Studio); *Yes Prime Minister* (Gielgud); *Scrabble* (DryWrite/Latitude); *I Caught Crabs in Walberswick* (Eastern Angles/High Tide/UK tour); *The Hothouse* (National Theatre); *Sleeve Notes,* (The Apathists/Theatre503) and *The Most Humane Way To Kill A Lobster* (Young Vic/Theatre503). Television credits include *EastEnders, Doctors, The Bill, Dream Team, A Touch of Frost, Judge John Deed, Family Affairs, Second Sight,* and *50 Ways To Kill Your Lover.* Film credits include *Women & Children* and *Enigma.*

CREATIVE TEAM

RUSSELL BENDER (Director)
Russell trained at Ecole Jacques Lecoq and on the 2010 Lincoln Center
Theater Directors' Lab. His work as a director includes *Kiss of the Earth*
(Concert Theatre, 25 venue UK tour); *The Shroud* by Siddartha Bose (Rich
Mix/Norfolk and Norwich Festival); *Game of Life* by Rose Lewenstein (The
Yard); *Emo* by Tom Wainwright (ATC/Bristol Old Vic Young Company/
Young Vic). In 2011 he was a staff director at the National Theatre. He has
assisted directors including Simon McBurney, Bijan Sheibani and Tom
Morris. He was a runner up of the 2009 JMK Award for young directors.
Outside of his theatre work, Russell has eight years' experience as a
software developer writing web and mobile applications for a number of
highly successful technology startups. He was a senior developer at
Spektrix, a leading cloud-based box office management software for the
arts, and does freelance consultancy for Patients Know Best, the world's
first fully patient-controlled online medical-records system.

ED BORGNIS (Production Manager)
Ed is a Production Manager working in the UK and worldwide. Recent
projects include *Impossible* world tour for Jamie Hendry Productions;
Calculating Kindness for Undercurrent; *Black and Gold*, Google's 2015
Christmas Party at the Roundhouse; *Grand Hotel* for Danielle Taranto and a
series of *Star Wars* launch events for HP. Ed has worked for the sound
departments for the RSC, Royal Ballet, Regent's Park Open Air,
Shakespeare's Globe, Tricycle, and various concert venues. He also dabbles
in video design. Ed has a Postgraduate Engineering degree from University
of Warwick and grew up in London and Norfolk.

HENRY GARNER (Creative Technologist)
Henry Garner has spent the last eight years working in the field of big data
analytics. For four years he was director and chief technologist of his own
medium-sized business providing marketing advice to multinational
companies and government organisations based on crunching large
quantities of user website data. He's currently a freelance consultant and
has recently published a book on data science and machine learning. His
background is in fine art, however, and he also helps artists realise their
creative visions with technology. He's done so in locations as diverse as
the Tate Britain, Great Eastern Hotel and the Cicely Saunders Institute,
most recently collaborating with Potential Difference on *Still* by The Future
is Unwritten (Ovalhouse).

JENNIFER JACKSON (Movement Director)
Jennifer trained at East15 and is an actor and movement director.
Movement direction includes *Why the Whales Came* (Danyah Miller &
Wizard Presents); *Debris* (Southwark Playhouse/Openworks Theatre); *Silent
Planet* (Finborough); *Macbeth* (Sam Wanamaker Playhouse); *Pericles*

(Berwaldhallen); *Subterranean Sepoys* (New Diorama). Jennifer was the assistant movement director on the Paines Plough Roundabout season 2014 (Fringe First winners), and is an associate artist with OpenWorks Theatre. Theatre includes *And Now: The World!* (Openworks Theatre/Derby Theatre); *Scenes from an Execution* (National Theatre); *Thérèse Raquin* (Bath Theatre Royal); *Death and the Maiden* (West End); *Humbug, Flathampton* (Royal & Derngate; winner of Argus Angel for Artistic Excellence at Brighton Festival 2013); *Macbeth* (Sam Wanamaker Playhouse); *Sonnet Walks* (Shakespeare's Globe); *Soon Until Forever, Red Shoes* (Theatre503); *Amphibians, The Drawing Play* (Offstage Theatre); *The Crunch* (Look Left Look Right); *Fixer* (Ovalhouse); *Moshing* (Arcola); *All That is Solid Melts Into Air* (National Theatre/Tangled Feet).

ROSE LEWENSTEIN (Writer)

Rose's plays include: *Now This Is Not The End* (Arcola); *Game of Life* (The Yard); *Only Human* (Theatre503); *Entries on Love* (Rich Mix) and *Ain't No Law Against Fish 'n' Chips* (Royal Court Young Writers Festival). Her latest play *Psychoslut* was featured in the Women@RADA series. Rose has been a member of the Royal Court's Supergroup and Young Writers Programme.

EDWARD LEWIS (Sound Designer)

Recent theatre includes *The Rubenstein Kiss* (Nottingham Playhouse); *Gravity* (Birmingham Rep); *A Midsummer Night's Dream* (Almeida); *Molly Sweeney and Thom Pain* (Print Room); *On the Rocks, Amongst Friends, Ignorance, Darker Shores* (Hampstead); *The Speed Twins, Slowly, Hurts Given and Received, Apple Pie* (Riverside Studios); *Baddies, Cuckoo, The Nutcracker, Britain's Best Recruiting Sergeant, The Caucasian Chalk Circle, Breaking the Ice, Hannah* (Unicorn); *Measure for Measure* (Cardiff Sherman); *Emo* (Bristol Old Vic/ Young Vic); *Once Upon a Time in Wigan, 65 Miles* (Paines Plough/ Hull Truck); *Krapp's Last Tape, Spoonface Steinberg* (Hull Truck); *The Shallow End* (Southwark Playhouse); *I Am Falling* (Sadler's Wells/The Gate, Notting Hill); *Orpheus and Eurydice, Quartet* (Old Vic Tunnels); *The Cement Garden* (The Vaults); *Abigail's Party, Pereira's Bakery, OK Tata Bye Bye* (Leicester Curve); *The Beloved* (Bush); *Chef* (Soho); *The Stronger, The Pariah, Boy With a Suitcase, Walking the Tightrope, Le Marriage, Meetings* (Arcola); *Hedda, Breathing Irregular* (The Gate, Notting Hill); *Madness in Valencia* (Trafalgar Studios); *Margaret Thatcher Queen of Soho* (Leicester Square); *The Madness of George III, Kalagora, Macbeth* (national tours); *The Separation* (Project Arts, Dublin); *Almost, Maine* (Park); *Othello* (Rose, Bankside); *Knives in Hens* (Battersea Arts Centre); *Personal Enemy* (White Bear/New York); *Cuddles, Milk Milk Lemonade, Full Circle* (Ovalhouse); *The Dazzle, Bug* (Found 111).

BENJAMIN LUKE (Company Stage Manager)

Benjamin is a stage and production manager based in London. He recently stage-managed the West End and Broadway run of *The Gruffalo* (Tall Stories) as well as its world tour. He has also worked with Tall Stories on *The Snow Dragon* at The St. James Theatre. Other stage management credits include *Macbeth* (Barbican R&D); *Around the World in*

80 Days and *Walking the Tightrope* (Arcola). His production management credits include *Macbeth* (Omnibus); *Take Me With You* UK tour (Starving Artists) and Production Management Apprentice abroad Celebrity Cruises.

KENDALL MASSON (Associate Producer)

Kendall Masson is a freelance arts fundraiser and producer. Whilst in London, Kendall was the Administrator and Events Manager for the Olivier Award-winning Actors Touring Company under Artistic Director Bijan Sheibani and an Events Manager at Timebased Events, a creative event production company. As a fundraiser, Kendall has recently worked with Convergence London (music + art + technology festival), Village Underground, Riotous Company, Told by an Idiot, Di Mainstone, Tonic Theatre, Association of Lighting Designers.

MILA SANDERS (Designer)

Her designs include *Love, Bombs and Apples* (Arcola); *Soapbox* (Talawa); *The Flannelettes* (King's Head); *Game of Life* (The Yard); *Queen of the Nile* (Hull Truck); *Dogs Barking* (RADA); *Parallax, The Door Never Closes, All the Little Things We Crushed* (Almeida); *The Only Way is Chelsea*'s (Root Theatre/ York Theatre Royal); *The Rite of Spring / Romeo and Juliet* (Concert Theatre); *Snakes and Ladders* (Rolemop); *Jelly Bean Jack* (Little Angel); *Pub Quiz* (New Writing North); *A Midsummer Night's Dream* (NT Education). As Costume Designer: *Macbeth, Twelfth Night* (NT Discover); *Tombstone Tales and Boothill Ballads* (Arcola); *Jason and the Argonauts* (BAC/tour); *Unfolding Andersen* (Theatre-rites).

BENJAMIN WALDEN (Video Designer)

Benjamin is a Brighton-based video artist and analogue animator experimenting within traditional methods. These include hand-drawn animations, film photography, low-gauge cine-film and early video. As well as theatrical and live collaborations Benjamin also creates music videos, short films and promotional content.

KATHARINE WILLIAMS (Lighting Designer)

Katharine Williams is a lighting designer for live performance. She works in the UK and internationally. Her designs have been seen in China, Hong Kong, New Zealand, Canada, the USA, Mexico, Ireland, Holland, Spain, Italy, Germany, Armenia, Romania, Russia and the Czech Republic. As a filmmaker, she is currently collaborating with Clare Duffy on Extreme Light North. Katharine is lead artist on the *Love Letters to the Home Office* project which campaigns using art, words and theatre to stop the means-tested tiering of Human Rights that is currently in place in the UK for international families. She is the founder of the Crew for Calais initiative, which gives creative industry professionals the opportunity to use their skills in the refugee camps in northern France.

potential difference

Potential Difference makes theatre of stories which communicate complex theoretical ideas and their impact on the world around us. Writers, directors and designers collaborate and consult with academics and specialists, so that their rigour and passion can inform the story, characters and staging. Our unusual creative process aims to make theatre that is viscerally and intellectually engaging and challenges the divide between sciences and arts. We also provide creative technology consultancy for theatre and other innovative creative projects.

www.potentialdifference.org.uk
hello@potentialdifference.org.uk
Registered Charity Number: 1166204

THANK YOUS

Darknet was developed with support of East15 Acting School, Battersea Arts Centre and Cambridge Junction. Thanks to: Andrea Brooks and students of East15 Acting School; Dr Alan Blackwell; Rosalie White, Sarah Golding and all at Battersea Arts Centre; Daniel Pitt at Cambridge Junction; Nicola Buckley, Hannah Smith, Mark Cartwright; and the artists and performers who were involved in development workshops: Esh Alladi, Alex Austin, Robin Berry, Cristina Catalina, Jennifer Jackson, Bettrys Jones, Nicholas Karimi, Avye Leventis, Helena Lymbery, Adam Pleeth, Mila Sanders, Moj Taylor, Mark Weinman.

We're hugely grateful to the many experts and specialists who gave their time helping us understand the intricacies of data sharing and cybersecurity. Including: Prof. Ross Anderson, Julie Broome, Jamie Bartlett, EJ Kroll, Dr Audrey Guinchard, Greg Jones, David Hendon, Dr Jens Jensen, Ken McAllum, Nathalie Nahai, Sir David Omand, Prof. Thomas Rid, Geoff White, Glenn Wilkinson.

Thanks to everyone who helped *Darknet* come to production: Chris Smyrnios, Alys Mayer, Richard Seary and all at Southwark Playhouse; Emily Coleman, the Potential Difference Board, Penny Clark, Brian Bender, Becca Heorton, Miles Otway.

Darknet would not have been possible without the generous support of: Bill Allan and Laura Swift, Robert and Jane Avery, Brian Bender, David Bender, Kenneth Bodman, Colin Budd, Kishan Chandarana, Rodney and Stephanie Clark, Malinda Coleman, Rachel Greene, Yvonne Horsfall-Turner, Gary Jones, Ligia Osepciu, John and Sarah Rhodes.

Supported using public funding by
ARTS COUNCIL
LOTTERY FUNDED **ENGLAND**

DARKNET

Rose Lewenstein

Acknowledgements

Chris Smyrnios and everyone at Southwark Playhouse, Harriet Pennington Legh, Becca Kinder, Nathalie Nahaï, Jamie Bartlett, Geoff White, Glenn Wilkinson, Greg Jones, Thomas Rid, David Omand, Ligia Osepciu, Wendy Kibble, Mark Lewenstein and Oliver Brierley.

Thanks to the actors and creatives who workshopped previous versions of the play: Esh Alladi, Alex Austin, Robin Berry, Cristina Catalina, Jennifer Jackson, Bettrys Jones, Nicholas Karimi, Helena Lymbery, Moj Taylor, Mark Weinman, William Drew, Avye Leventis, Adam Pleeth and Mila Sanders.

Special thanks to Russell Bender, without whom this play wouldn't have been written.

R.L.

4

Characters
in order of seen or heard

VOICE-OVER
JAMIE
STEVE
CONSULTANT
STACEY
GARY
ALLEN
KYLA
DONNY D
AUTOMATED VOICE
COUNSELLOR
GIRLS' VOICES
CHARLOTTE
CANDY/NATALIA
HACKDOLZ
EMPLOYEES
MITCH
JOHN
JOURNALISTS
ELEKTRA
VENDORS
HEISENBERG
BUYERS
STUDIO HACKERS
REPORTERS
SCHOOLGIRLS
DAVID
VOICES
DOCTOR X
PARAMEDICS
NURSE
VALERIE
MR PR

MS FINANCE
POLICEMEN
JUDGE
PROSECUTORS
LAWYERS
CLERK
MR MOSEDALE
RACHEL

Notes

Nothing about the play is naturalistic.

Scenes don't stop and start but jump from one to another, as though the audience are navigating multiple web pages.

There is a stark difference between offline and online. Laptops and other devices are also used as light sources and as a means of communicating textual and visual information.

The play can be doubled. Obvs.

This text went to press before the end of rehearsals and so may differ slightly from the play as performed.

PART ONE

*Darkness. A promotional video plays. It begins with a digital
octopus. Tentacles reach across various screens. Simple visuals
illustrate the message.*

VOICE-OVER. Money doesn't make the world go round.
You do.

So if you are what you do and you say who you are then why
shouldn't you get something in return?

No more giving it away for free. No more watching others
profit from what is yours.

When you share data with Octopus, our algorithms calculate
the real-time market value and transfer it straight to your
Octopay wallet.

The more you share, the more you earn.

You're rolling in data. Spend it wisely.

The octopus smiles and winks, then disappears.

JAMIE *sits alone in his bedroom, staring straight ahead,
hands flat on top of his laptop.* STEVE *stands on the other
side of a door.*

STEVE. Jamie?

Jamie can I have a word?

I've just had a phone call from Mr Mosedale.

He said *somebody* replaced the school homepage with a
photograph of a penis.

He's not very happy.

I told him innocent until proven guilty but he seems to think
you're the only student who could do that sort of thing.

Jamie?

I'm only going to ask you once. Did you or did you not replace the school homepage with a photograph of a penis?

And no you do not have the right to remain silent.

Look, if you refuse to even answer the question then I'm going to have to assume you're guilty.

Jamie if you don't open the door –

STEVE *opens the door and enters the bedroom.*

Right, that's it, you're grounded.

JAMIE *doesn't respond.*

And I'm confiscating your computer until you've apologised to Mr Mosedale.

JAMIE *takes his hands off the laptop.* STEVE *picks it up, pauses for a moment, then leaves.* JAMIE *immediately produces another laptop and opens it.*

A clinic. STACEY *is visibly shaking. A* CONSULTANT *takes notes on a device.*

CONSULTANT. First of all let me say that the fact you've made the step to come here today and ask for help is a really positive start.

STACEY. Okay.

CONSULTANT. So I'm going to go through a few options with you.

STACEY. Okay.

CONSULTANT. So we offer behavioural therapy or prescribed medication, or in some cases a combination of the two.

STACEY. Okay.

CONSULTANT. We find a combination is usually the most effective.

STACEY. Okay.

CONSULTANT. *Are* you okay?

STACEY. Yeah.

CONSULTANT.

STACEY. I just want it as soon as possible.

CONSULTANT. Have you taken a course of methadone before?

STACEY. No.

CONSULTANT. And are you aware of the terms and conditions?

STACEY. But the ad said –

CONSULTANT. The treatment is free, yes, but it'll be linked to your Octopus ID and so your data will be shared with third-party companies.

It's still confidential of course.

STACEY. But –

CONSULTANT.

STACEY. Won't it affect my score?

CONSULTANT. Well, yes, it may, in the short term, impact on your Octoscore.

STACEY. So –

CONSULTANT.

STACEY. Won't my value go down?

CONSULTANT. Well, yes, you could see an initial drop in the value of your data.

STACEY. Okay.

CONSULTANT. But we do still recommend customers go ahead with the treatment. Once you've been clean for a year you'll start to see an improvement.

STACEY. Okay.

CONSULTANT. The full T and Cs are attached to your appointment card.

STACEY. Okay.

CONSULTANT. Okay, if I could start by taking a few details –

STACEY gets up.

STACEY. I've gotta –

She looks towards the door.

CONSULTANT. It really is for the best in the long run.

STACEY. Yeah. Thanks. I'll think about it.

She leaves.

A prison visiting room. ALLEN and GARY sit across from one another at a table.

GARY. I'm not interested.

ALLEN. Just hear me out.

GARY. You know how long I got?

ALLEN. Well, sure, but we all know life doesn't actually mean *life*.

GARY. How about when you multiply it by nine?

ALLEN. Nine life sentences? What do they think you are, a cat?

Prison cat meme: KITTENS, YOU DON'T GET PAROLE FOR BAD BEHAVIOUR.

GARY. They reckon hackers are a greater danger to society than rapists and murderers.

ALLEN. Well, maybe they are.

GARY.

ALLEN. I'm kidding. I happen to have a great deal of respect for hackers. Wouldn't be here if I didn't.

GARY.

ALLEN. Okay listen, Gary – do I call you Gary or Houdini?

GARY. Gary's fine.

ALLEN. Gary, you did a bad thing and they're using you as an example. But I wouldn't be here if I wasn't confident our lawyers had a strong case for early release –

GARY. If I work for you.

ALLEN. If you work *with* us.

GARY. You realise the purpose of Kyla was to fuck with companies like Octopus.

ALLEN. I am aware of that.

GARY. So working with you or for you just goes against all my reasons for creating it in the first place.

Just seems fundamentally unethical.

ALLEN. It wasn't exactly ethical of you to steal masses of personal data and then dump it in the public domain.

GARY. Yeah, well, seems like your ethics and my ethics are a bit different.

ALLEN. Bottom line is you can rot in here for the rest of your life or you can sign a statement that says you'll work with us on release.

Your talent is wasted in here. But you have the chance to turn things around. Competitive salary, shares in the company, a shiny new reputation –

You have a family, right?

GARY *doesn't respond.*

KYLA *arrives home, still wearing school uniform. She finds* STACEY *passed out, arm bloated and covered in red marks.*

A TV show plays on a screen.

DONNY D. Hello and welcome to *You've Been Doxxed!* with me, Donny D.

Canned applause from the studio audience.

KYLA *turns it off with a remote.*

KYLA. Mum?

She shakes STACEY *awake.*

Mum?

STACEY. What time is it?

KYLA. Teatime.

STACEY searches the floor for cash.

STACEY. I need you to get something for me.

KYLA. Mum, your arm's all swollen.

She finds the cash and hands it to KYLA.

STACEY. Ask for Mitch, yeah?

KYLA. Mum, it's not s'posed to do that.

STACEY. You know where to find him, yeah?

KYLA. Is that his stuff you've done, 'cause that's not normal, that's not s'posed to happen.

STACEY. Just go and get it and I'll make you some tea.

KYLA. Will you?

STACEY. Yeah.

KYLA. With what?

STACEY. Don't pick a fight with me, why you always picking a fight with me?

KYLA. Because I'm hungry and because you're killing yourself.

STACEY.

KYLA.

STACEY. Alright.

KYLA. Alright what.

STACEY. I'll get it myself.

She tries to stand and immediately falls back down.

KYLA. Right, I'm calling –

STACEY. No.

KYLA. Mum.

STACEY. You know what happens if you call. They take you away from me. Is that what you want?

KYLA. I want you to get better.

STACEY. I'm trying.

KYLA. Are you?

STACEY. I went to the clinic.

KYLA. And?

STACEY. They can't help me.

KYLA. Why not?

STACEY. It's complicated.

KYLA.

STACEY. My score's already rock bottom. Food, bills – you know how it works, if it goes any lower there won't be enough.

KYLA.

STACEY. I tried, alright?

KYLA. Well I'm not gonna let you give up.

KYLA *leaves with the cash*.

STACEY. Wait –

ALLEN *stands up*.

ALLEN. I fly back tomorrow morning. Think about it.

GARY. Wait.

ALLEN *sits back down*.

Why me?

ALLEN. Because if you're able to infiltrate our networks then you're also able to make them more secure.

GARY. That's it?

ALLEN. You know our systems, you know our algorithms –

Octopus needs minds like yours. I'm not asking you to sit in an office and take orders. I'm asking you to help us build something beautiful.

You write brilliant malware. Write brilliant software instead.

GARY. Give me an example.

ALLEN. Alright. So for example we're developing predictive ordering –

GARY. Predictive ordering?

ALLEN. That's a working title but essentially it's finding and comparing the best deals on the market and ordering on behalf of the user.

GARY. Eliminating choice.

ALLEN. Actually the decisions our algorithms make are far more representative of individual preferences than those we make ourselves. It's all based on user profiles.

GARY. What kind of decisions you talking about?

ALLEN. Energy tariffs, insurance policies, home improvements, vacation packages, nose jobs – I'm kidding, I'm kidding about the nose jobs – but I dunno, we're a forward-thinking company, and maybe, eventually –

GARY. Maybe, eventually, no one will ever have to make a single conscious choice again.

ALLEN *ignores the interjection.*

ALLEN. Anyway, to do all that effectively we need to find new ways of cross-referencing multiple sets of data. Obviously this is some ways off, and obviously we're not the only company doing this sort of thing –

GARY. It's a race.

ALLEN. It's business.

GARY. And you think you can win it by hiring a convicted criminal.

ALLEN. People change. Yesterday you were the great Houdini –

GARY. Houdini's an avatar.

ALLEN. Right, and today you're just plain old Gary White. Question is, who do you want to be tomorrow?

GARY *looks down at the table*.

Well?

GARY. I'm thinking.

ALLEN. Bottom line is we work with the brightest minds in the world and we think you've got one of them. That's why I'm here. But if you can't get on board with our ethos –

GARY. I'm still thinking.

ALLEN. Alright, good.

Thinking is good.

And you know, I like the fact you're a man of strong convictions. Sure, I think those convictions are wrong – illegal, in fact – but I like it all the same. I'm always saying to Charlotte –

GARY *looks up*.

GARY. Who's Charlotte?

ALLEN. Oh, we're trialling this new virtual PA system. You'll get one too if you –

Anyway, and so I find myself joking with her that I'd wish she'd just have a goddamn opinion about something, you know?

GARY.

ALLEN. Like, I dunno, what colour tie I should wear or how to speak to women without objectifying them –

GARY. But Charlotte doesn't think, Charlotte doesn't have an opinion, because Charlotte's not a human.

ALLEN. Right. And I like humans, you know?

KYLA *sits on a bench, ear to her phone, waiting in a queue*.

AUTOMATED VOICE. Please hold the line. Your call will be answered shortly. If your call is an emergency please hang up and dial –

COUNSELLOR. Thank you for holding, you're through to *Help*, my name is Carol, how can I *help* you?

KYLA. It's not me, it's my mum.

I just, um –

I just want to know if it's normal – I mean, for people who – you know –

Arms. Is it normal for arms to swell up?

COUNSELLOR. Can I go through a checklist with you?

KYLA. Um, yeah, alright.

COUNSELLOR. Are you with your mum at the moment?

KYLA. No, I'm on a bench in the park.

COUNSELLOR. Yes, I can see your location.

KYLA. What?

COUNSELLOR. Your GPS Coordinates have been automatically enabled in case of emergency.

KYLA. But I thought calls were anonymous.

COUNSELLOR. Calls *are* anonymous.

KYLA. I thought that was the point.

COUNSELLOR. I don't currently have access to your name and Octopus ID, but if the information you provide suggests that either you or your mum are in danger then I'm legally obliged to transfer your details to –

KYLA *hangs up and stares at her phone*.

GIRLS' VOICES. Her mum is a junkie whore lol.

Ten ways to tie your hair in a ponytail.

No laughing matter but lol.

Look at this kitten massaging this puppy ohmygod cuuute.

ALLEN *leans in closer.*

ALLEN. I know what you're thinking.

GARY. Yeah?

ALLEN. You're thinking about life outside. How long's it been? Three years? Four?

GARY. That's not what I was thinking about.

ALLEN. A lot's changed.

GARY. Yeah.

ALLEN. Four years in tech, that's like –

GARY. Yeah, I know.

ALLEN. What's that in cat years, like sixteen?

Shocked cat meme: YOU'RE HOW OLD?!?!

GARY. Show me the statement.

ALLEN produces a bound paper contract and lays it on the table. GARY flicks through it.

And I'd get a Charlotte?

ALLEN. Sure. Ed lets you pick the name.

GARY. Who's Ed?

ALLEN. Ed Simpson, lead developer, you'd like him.

GARY continues to flick through the contract. Finally, he looks up at ALLEN.

GARY. Got a pen?

ALLEN. Uh, pen, yes, right –

ALLEN finds a pen in his pocket and hands it to GARY.

GARY. I could stab you with this.

For a split second it's almost as though he might. Then GARY grins, shakes his head, and signs on the dotted line.

JAMIE is hunched over this laptop, typing furiously. KYLA and STEVE stand on the other side of a door.

STEVE. Jamie?

JAMIE *stops, closes his laptop and places his hands flat on top of it.*

There's a *girl* here to see you.

JAMIE. Tell her I'm grounded.

STEVE. Oh I did.

KYLA *looks at* STEVE.

She says it's important.

STEVE *winks at* KYLA.

Jamie?

You didn't tell me you had a girlfriend.

JAMIE. I don't have a girlfriend.

KYLA (*to* STEVE). I'm not his girlfriend.

STEVE. Alright, but you didn't tell me you had a girl *friend*.

KYLA (*to* STEVE). We're not friends.

STEVE. Jamie, is this something to do with the penis?

(*To* KYLA.) I'm sorry, sweetheart –

KYLA. My name's not sweetheart, it's Kyla.

JAMIE *hears* KYLA *say her name and looks towards the door.*

STEVE. Well I'm sorry, Kyla, but my son is a rather *asocial* creature, as you might have noticed. When I was sixteen I'd have jumped at the chance to have a girl like you in my bedroom.

KYLA.

STEVE. But I'm not sixteen. And I probably shouldn't say things like that.

JAMIE. Tell her she can come in.

STEVE *turns in surprise.*

STEVE. Right. Well. Be safe.

I mean –

In life. Generally.

A hotel room. ALLEN *holds the signed contract.*

CHARLOTTE. How was your day?

ALLEN. Very productive. Thank you, Charlotte.

CHARLOTTE. You're welcome.

Bad weather we're having.

ALLEN. English people like the rain.

CHARLOTTE. Is that a joke?

ALLEN. Uh, no, I mean, yes, I don't know, it just came out.

CHARLOTTE. Would you like me to go through your diary?

ALLEN. Sure, go ahead.

CHARLOTTE. Flight departing LHR at zero six forty local time, arriving SFO at zero seven forty-five local time.

You're checked into a window seat and I've ordered you the rainbow salad.

Presentation at Octopus Inc. HQ yellow room commencing zero nine thirty.

Your notes and slides will be available to edit inflight.

Press conference at Octopus Inc. HQ purple room commencing –

ALLEN. Thank you, Charlotte, that's enough for now.

CHARLOTTE. You're welcome.

Can I help you with anything else?

ALLEN. You hungry? Want room service?

CHARLOTTE. Is that a joke?

ALLEN. Yes, that was a joke, because you don't eat.

CHARLOTTE. Are *you* hungry? Do *you* want room service?

ALLEN. I'm thinking about ordering the beef lasagne.

CHARLOTTE. There are seven hundred and twenty-six calories in the beef lasagne.

ALLEN. Oh. Is that a lot?

CHARLOTTE. The recommended daily calorie intake for the average male is two thousand five hundred.

ALLEN. Okay, so –

CHARLOTTE. The beef lasagne is thirty-four point four eight per cent of your recommended daily calorie intake.

ALLEN. Could you turn off the double decimals please?

CHARLOTTE. Sure.

ALLEN. Okay, so are you saying I *shouldn't* order the beef lasagne?

CHARLOTTE. Based on your age, body mass index, activity levels, adrenaline levels and ecological footprint, I would advise you *not* to order the beef lasagne.

ALLEN. Thank you, Charlotte.

CHARLOTTE. You're welcome.

JAMIE *stares at* KYLA. *His hands are still flat on top of his laptop.*

KYLA. Alright, Jamie?

JAMIE *doesn't respond.*

Um, yeah, I couldn't find you on MyCloud so –

JAMIE. I'm not on MyCloud.

KYLA. So yeah, I thought I'd just, um, come to your house.

I know you probably don't know me 'cause no one in year eleven knows anyone in year nine but –

But yeah, I know you, I mean I know of you – sorry, don't mean to be all like stalkery – but yeah, you're the one who did the penis thing, aren't you.

That was so funny.

JAMIE. It wasn't a joke.

KYLA. Oh. What was it then?

JAMIE. A protest.

KYLA. Oh. Okay.

So, um, why aren't you on MyCloud?

JAMIE. Because I don't believe in the privatisation of data.

KYLA. That's cool.

JAMIE. You know that everything you say and do now on MyCloud will be factored into your Octoscore when you turn eighteen.

KYLA. Yeah, well, that's ages away.

I only post pictures of cats anyway.

Bread cat meme: FEAR ME, FOR I AM IN BREAD.

JAMIE. Their algorithms suggest that moderate viewing of cat pictures can actually improve your score, but that excessive viewing of cat pictures has a negative impact.

KYLA. What counts as excessive?

JAMIE. Depends on the average number of cat pictures being viewed at any one time.

KYLA. But you don't share anything.

JAMIE. No.

KYLA. So your score's gonna be shit.

JAMIE. Yeah.

KYLA. So how you gonna pay for like food and bills and stuff?

JAMIE *ignores the question.*

JAMIE. Did you know you're named after the most sophisticated virus ever created?

KYLA. Um, no?

JAMIE. Well you are.

KYLA. Okay.

JAMIE. Although Kyla is less than five years old and you're –

KYLA. Fourteen.

JAMIE. So it's more like the virus is named after you.

KYLA. I thought it was Gaelic or something.

JAMIE.

KYLA. Anyway, yeah, so seeing as you did the penis thing –

I thought maybe you could help me with something.

JAMIE. I'm busy.

KYLA. Oh. Okay.

What you busy with?

JAMIE. None of your business.

KYLA. No. Yeah. Sorry.

But actually it's kind of important.

Like, life-or-death important.

JAMIE *doesn't respond.*

I'll just wait, shall I?

KYLA *sits down and gets out her phone.*

GIRLS' VOICES. She's never had a proper boyfriend lol.

Seven ways to deal with girls hitting on your man.

She's never even had sex lol.

Save Timmy the Tiger.

ALLEN *opens his laptop, then looks towards* CHARLOTTE.

ALLEN. I'm sorry, I know you don't judge, but I'm just not comfortable having another female presence in the room while I –

Not that I'm planning to –

I don't even know why I'm trying to explain myself.

I'm turning you off, Charlotte.

CHARLOTTE. Goodnight, Allen.

CHARLOTTE *disappears*.

ALLEN *clicks on an image of a girl and* CANDY *appears on his screen. She wears cheap garish underwear, a wig and lots of make-up. A smile is glued to her face.*

ALLEN. Candy?

CANDY. Hello?

ALLEN. Is that a, uh, common Romanian forename?

CANDY.

ALLEN. You know, in America the word *candy* means confectionary.

CANDY. Yes?

ALLEN. Do you speak English?

CANDY. A little.

ALLEN. You're very pretty.

CANDY. Thank you.

I take clothes off now?

ALLEN. Oh, uh, no, not yet.

Tell me something about yourself.

CANDY. Me?

ALLEN. What do you like to do?

CANDY. Striptease?

ALLEN. No, I mean in real life.

CANDY. You know this is cam site?

ALLEN. Yes, I know what it is.

CANDY. You pay per minute?

ALLEN. Yes, I'm happy to pay.

CANDY. Yes?

ALLEN. Yes, I'm just trying to get to know you a little bit.

CANDY.

ALLEN. So do you have any hobbies?

CANDY. Hobbies?

ALLEN. Things you do for fun? Other than striptease?

CANDY. Yes, I study history of art.

ALLEN. Oh. Wow.

CANDY. I like paintings.

ALLEN. That's great. I like paintings too.

CANDY. Yes?

ALLEN. I have a few on my walls back home.

CANDY. Yes?

ALLEN. You heard of Seurat?

CANDY. Of course.

ALLEN. I have a Seurat on my wall.

CANDY. Yes?

ALLEN. I'll be honest, Candy, I don't know a whole lot about *art* but I like looking at that painting. I like how when you go right up close it's thousands of tiny dots and then you step back and –

CANDY. Is because brain is send message to eyes and – sorry, my English is not –

ALLEN. No, I get it, the brain sends a message to the eyes and suddenly you can see the bigger picture.

CANDY. Yes.

ALLEN (*to himself*). Bigger picture. I like that.

> KYLA *puts her phone away.* JAMIE*'s hands are still flat on top of his laptop.*

KYLA. Why are you covering it with your hands like that?

Are you autistic or something?

JAMIE. No.

KYLA. I'm not gonna steal it.

JAMIE. I know. I'm waiting for you to leave.

KYLA.

JAMIE.

KYLA. Most boys try and have sex with me if I come into their bedroom but you won't even talk to me.

JAMIE. Did you want to have sex?

KYLA. Um, no?

JAMIE. Good.

KYLA. Good?

JAMIE. Yeah.

KYLA. Thanks.

JAMIE. You're fourteen.

KYLA. Yeah, well, bet it wouldn't be the first time you broke the law.

    JAMIE *stares at her.*

JAMIE. What do you want?

KYLA. Methadone.

JAMIE.

KYLA. I heard there's places you can get whatever you want without leaving a trace.

    I heard you just need the right browser or something but I don't have a computer and –

JAMIE. You don't have a computer?

KYLA. I did have one from school but my mum sold it so I've only got my phone and GPS Coordinates is always on.

    And anyway, our internet's always getting cut off, so she can't share as much or earn as much and –

And anyway, I'd have to learn how to do it and I don't want *how to buy drugs on the deep web* to show up on my history.

It's not for me, it's for –

JAMIE. You don't have to tell me, it's none of my business.

KYLA. No. Yeah. Everyone knows.

It's my mum. Her arm's swollen up. It's that street stuff she gets, it's cut to shit. Anyway, she tried to get help but she won't get methadone on prescription 'cause –

JAMIE. It lowers her Octoscore.

KYLA. Yeah. Something like that. She said it's complicated. But yeah.

I got cash.

KYLA *pulls the cash out her pocket and holds it out to him.*

Please, Jamie.

I don't want her to die.

She looks like she might cry, but doesn't.

ALLEN *is mid-story.* CANDY *listens.*

ALLEN. No, and so, yeah, that was how it was, no contact with the outside world. No telephones, no computers – according to my father, technology was the work of the devil. And I guess I never questioned it until one day – I must've been nine or ten, something like that – but one day I took a wrong turn on the way back from Sunday School and I walked past what I later learned to be an electrical store, and in the window of the store was a display of about twenty television sets, all piled on top of one another, each showing the same weather forecast.

Sunshine. It was a heat wave. I remember that.

And so anyway, I stood there, mesmerised – could've been hours, minutes, seconds, I'd never seen a TV before in my life – but anyway I stood there in some kind of trance until eventually my father caught up with me and dragged, literally, dragged me by the ear, all the way home. And later he tried to *beat* the devil out of me like some sort of exorcism but it was too late. Because at that point I knew. I didn't know what I knew but I knew I knew something. *Possibility.*

I suppose what I now believe – well, that's almost a religion in itself. At least, that's how I approach it.

To this day I still wonder what might've happened to me if I hadn't taken that wrong turn.

CANDY.

ALLEN. I'm sorry, I –

CANDY. No, is good to talk.

ALLEN. Yeah. It *is* good to talk.

Well, it was nice meeting you, Candy.

CANDY. I take clothes off now?

ALLEN. No. I mean, thank you, but no. I'm sure it's, uh, very pretty under there but – sorry, that didn't come out right –

Anyway. It really was nice talking to you.

CANDY. I will see you again?

ALLEN. I would like that very much.

Goodnight, Candy.

He clicks and CANDY *disappears. He inhales on an e-cigarette.*

JAMIE looks at the cash.

JAMIE. You need to pay in that cash and buy cryptocoins.

KYLA. Okay.

JAMIE. It's too late now, the banks are shut.

KYLA. But –

JAMIE. Come back tomorrow.

He waits for her to leave.

KYLA. Okay.

She hesitates for a moment. They stare at each other.

Thanks, Jamie.

She leaves. He pauses, then opens his laptop.

ALLEN *receives an email alert.*

AUTOMATED VOICE. New message from Ed Simpson.

ALLEN *clicks on the email.*

Update available for Virtual PA.

Hi Allen. See below for latest update. Pretty excited about this one. As always, feedback appreciated. Ed.

He clicks on a link in the body of the email.

Update improves stability and performance, resolves an issue that could lead to doubling of information across devices and installs advanced human-interaction technology.

He clicks UPDATE.

Thumping disco music and flashing lights. Four HACKDOLZ enter. They wear neon balaclavas and long blonde Barbie-like hair. A stream of impenetrable programming language appears on various screens.

The music builds. Text and images jump from screen to screen. The HACKDOLZ break into the network.

In amongst all this, the sound of a plane taking off. The world spins on its axis. Lights flicker on and off – faulty strip lighting or night turning to day. A digital clock speeds up, turning hours to minutes to seconds until –

PART TWO

Lights up on Octopus Inc. HQ. ALLEN *addresses an audience of bright-eyed Octopus* EMPLOYEES.

ALLEN. In three hundred and fifty BC Aristotle said that every object had two uses, the first being the original purpose for which the object was designed, the second its possibility as an item to sell or barter. Those objects with the greatest utility were deemed the most valuable, and as people's needs became more refined so did their currency. Humans placed trust in exchanging metal for goods – gold, silver, bronze, copper – and then paper. Printed promises.

Nowadays the only people to use cold hard cash are digital immigrants and criminals. Your grandmother and your drug dealer. People who have something to hide. Nowadays most of you will go a whole lifetime without ever holding money in your hand. It goes into an account at the end of each month and you spend it via your phone or digital wallet. Money is no longer a tangible object. It is, for want of a better word, invisible.

But there's a new currency that's proving more valuable than any object. A currency that doesn't rely on the weight of gold or financial guarantees, that isn't tied to stock markets or credit or interest rates. A currency that grows with the population. A self-sustaining currency. A currency that doesn't run out.

That currency is data.

A council estate. STACEY *turns a corner and finds* MITCH.

STACEY. Alright, Mitch?

Did Kyla come down here last night?

MITCH. Who?

STACEY. Kyla, my daughter, she was meant to pick some stuff up for me.

MITCH. Nah.

STACEY. I gave her the cash.

MITCH. Yeah?

STACEY. Don't s'pose you'd give me some on tick –

MITCH. Do I look like a fucking charity?

STACEY. Just till she's back from school –

MITCH. Lovely fucking mother you are, sending your daughter out to pick up for you.

STACEY. Please, Mitch.

I can give you something else if you like.

You know. As interest.

ALLEN *continues his speech.*

ALLEN. I know I'm preaching to the converted here when I say that Octopay has been a game-changer for companies and users alike.

I used to joke that mainstream tech users fell into two camps: data whores and data cynics. Data whores were oblivious, they didn't care, they gave it away for free, and as a result they were often exploited. Then you had the data cynics, the ones who actively withheld their data, the ones who didn't trust anything that asked them to tick a box. And when you look at these two extremes – the whore and the cynic – you see that it really comes down to two things: informing the user and gaining their trust.

Octopay does just that. It incentivises users to share their data because the more they share, the more they're worth. And the more we know, the better service we can offer.

Which brings me to predictive ordering. Sure, we already have services trading in information, that's nothing new. I use a search engine to help me decide on which car I'm gonna buy. It figures I'm interested in cars. It sells my search to a bunch of companies who sell it to another bunch of companies who pay the search engine to fill up my sidebar with ads for the same car I just went out and bought. I use a social-media site to post a photo of me in my new car. It figures I'm a) interested in cars and b) like posing in cars. It combines my interest in cars and posing in cars with my age, gender, location, education, relationship status, et cetera, and sells all that to another bunch of companies who pay the social-media site to fill up my sidebar with more fucking ads for the very same car I just posted on my wall.

It's like waiting outside a burger joint to sell burgers to people who've just eaten burgers. You can understand why the data cynics got fed up of dumb targeted advertising, right?

But thanks to Octopay we can be a lot smarter. I don't need to wait outside a burger joint to find people who like burgers because Octopus knows whether you like burgers before you've even tried one. Octopus also knows when it's time to stop eating burgers and get on the treadmill. It knows which movie you wanna watch next weekend, it knows the best month to plan your wedding, it knows the optimum time to try for a baby, it knows what is best for you because it can see the *bigger picture*.

STACEY *grabs hold of* MITCH. *She is shaking.*

STACEY. Mitch, please.

MITCH. Thing is, Stace, you ain't got nothing that's worth nothing to me no more.

She kneels down and starts unbuttoning his trousers. He rolls his eyes but doesn't stop her.

As STACEY *gives* MITCH *a blow job,* ALLEN *continues his speech.*

ALLEN. And that picture is getting bigger and bigger. More users every day, more jobs created through our programmes, more connections made with companies and providers.

With new innovation comes fear of the unknown.

Why are we here? Why are we doing this? Because we give a damn about the future of our internet. We believe in equal access to services and information. We believe in giving everyone the opportunity to create their own wealth without taking it away from others. We believe in hope for a new generation of users.

The EMPLOYEES *burst into spontaneous applause.*
ALLEN *pauses as it dies down.*

I'm proud to say we work with some of the best minds in the country, if not the world. And that is where you come in.

So, uh, I'll stop talking now, apart from to say a big welcome to all the new faces joining us today for this exciting next chapter. Please make yourselves at home, get to know the campus, take advantage of the facilities – yoga, juice bar, chill-out zone –

Yeah. That's it. Welcome to Octopus.

STACEY *wipes her mouth and stands up.*

MITCH. Alright. Bring me the cash tonight.

STACEY. I will, I promise.

MITCH. All of it.

STACEY. I promise I will.

MITCH *hands her a wrap.*

MITCH. It's only 'cause I feel fucking sorry for you.

STACEY *leaves.*

ALLEN *enters his office and turns on* CHARLOTTE.

CHARLOTTE. Good morning, Allen.

ALLEN. Good morning.

CHARLOTTE. How are you today?

ALLEN. Jetlagged.

CHARLOTTE. You're welcome.

ALLEN. What?

CHARLOTTE. You're welcome.

ALLEN. No, I said –

Never mind. Stupid update.

CHARLOTTE. There are no available updates.

ALLEN. Well no, not any more, I updated you last night.

CHARLOTTE. There are no available updates.

ALLEN. I heard you, Charlotte.

CHARLOTTE. You're welcome.

ALLEN. Jesus.

CHARLOTTE. Is that a joke?

ALLEN. Jesus?

CHARLOTTE. Yes.

ALLEN. Is Jesus a joke?

CHARLOTTE. Are you asking me if Jesus is a joke?

ALLEN. What? No.

(*To himself.*) This is what they call advanced human-interaction technology?

CHARLOTTE. Can I help you with anything else?

ALLEN. Coffee would be great.

KYLA *arrives home. She finds* STACEY *passed out.*

The same TV show plays on a screen.

DONNY D. Are you ready to ruin someone's life?

Canned cheers from the studio audience.

That's the spirit. And remember: whatever happens here, there's always something worse happening on 4chan.

KYLA *turns it off with a remote.*

KYLA. Mum?

She shakes STACEY *awake.*

Mum?

STACEY. I'm a bad mother.

KYLA. What?

STACEY. I shouldn't have asked you to get it for me.

KYLA. It's alright.

STACEY. No it's not alright, I shouldn't have asked you, I shouldn't have done that, but listen, that cash I gave you, I need it back now, yeah?

GIRLS' VOICES. Her mum is a junkie whore lol.

KYLA. Mum, it's alright, I'm sorting it.

STACEY. I'm serious, Kyla, I need it back.

GIRLS' VOICES. No laughing matter but lol.

KYLA. I found a way to get it for you.

STACEY. Get what?

KYLA. Methadone.

STACEY. No, you don't understand –

KYLA. Just gotta wait a couple of days.

STACEY. The terms and conditions –

KYLA. It's not from the clinic and it won't affect your score.

STACEY.

KYLA.

STACEY. I need that money, Kyla.

KYLA. A couple of days, that's all.

STACEY. Kyla –

KYLA. I gotta go.

KYLA *leaves.*

STACEY. Wait –

ALLEN *is drinking coffee.* JOHN *enters.*

JOHN. Allen, mind if I –

ALLEN. No, please –

JOHN. Great speech.

ALLEN. Coffee?

JOHN. And how was – oh, no, thank you – how was London?

ALLEN *produces the bound paper contract and hands it to* JOHN.

He signed?

ALLEN. Told you he would.

JOHN. Can we trust him?

ALLEN. People change.

JOHN. Sure, no, it's just –

ALLEN. What?

JOHN. No, just, I'm sure it's all fine but –

ALLEN. But what?

JOHN. The directors are a little worried is all.

ALLEN. We agreed on this months ago.

JOHN. It's just if we were to lobby for his release –

ALLEN. If? He signed.

JOHN. Right, sure, but if, when, we do that –

ALLEN. We checked all this with legal.

JOHN. No, I know –

ALLEN. This isn't the first time a hacker's switched hats.

JOHN. I know, and I guess I'm coming at it from more of a PR perspective but –

ALLEN. I wasn't planning on announcing it to the press this afternoon if that's what you're saying.

JOHN. But at some point it's going to come out that the dude who wrote the deadliest virus known to man is coming to work for Octopus Inc.

ALLEN. What is not cool about that?

JOHN. I know, we're a forward-thinking company, but come on, that's like inviting the man who burgled your house round to dinner.

ALLEN. Sounds like the kinda thing Jesus would do.

JOHN.

ALLEN. Let's see what happens. Nine life sentences. It's always been a long shot.

JOHN. Nine life sentences? What do they think he is, a cat?

ALLEN. That's what *I* said.

JOHN. Jesus.

ALLEN. I know.

JOHN. Can you imagine?

ALLEN. What?

JOHN. Being locked up for nine lives?

ALLEN. Not really.

JOHN. Jesus.

JAMIE is hunched over his laptop, typing furiously. KYLA *and* STEVE *stand on the other side of a door.*

STEVE. Jamie?

(*To* KYLA.) I do worry sometimes, the amount of time he spends in that one room.

KYLA. Thought you said he was grounded.

STEVE. Yes, I didn't really think that through, did I.

(*To* JAMIE.) Jamie?

(*To* KYLA.) Perhaps I should've sent him out as punishment. Community service, something like that.

KYLA. I don't think dads are allowed to sentence their kids to community service.

STEVE. No, you're probably right. What would your father have done?

KYLA. I don't know, I've never met him.

STEVE. Oh I am sorry.

KYLA. No, it's okay, I don't care.

STEVE.

KYLA.

STEVE. So are you two –

He gestures towards JAMIE*'s room.*

KYLA. What?

STEVE. Dating or –

KYLA. Yeah, kind of.

STEVE. Oh.

Well I must say I'm quite relieved.

KYLA.

STEVE. I was starting to think he might be –

KYLA. What?

STEVE. You know –

KYLA. Gay?

STEVE. *Asexual.*

KYLA. Oh.

STEVE. A lot of young people are these days. They'd rather spend their time with a machine than with another human being.

KYLA.

STEVE. Well, as long as you're – you know –

KYLA.

STEVE. Safe.

KYLA. You mean condoms and stuff?

STEVE (*to* JAMIE). Jamie?

KYLA. I'm fourteen.

STEVE. Jamie, open the door.

> JAMIE *stops, closes his laptop and places his hands flat on top of it.*

> JOHN *turns to leave, then stops.*

JOHN. Oh, I meant to ask, how you getting on with Charlotte?

ALLEN. Uh, yeah, she's great. A real character.

JOHN. We're thinking of rolling them out to the whole of senior management, so any feedback –

ALLEN. Right, Ed mentioned that.

No, she's pretty intuitive.

Actually I think she made her first joke this morning.

JOHN. Huh. Didn't know they were programmed to do that.

ALLEN.

JOHN. Alright, well, I better –

ALLEN. Good talking to you, John.

JOHN. We're all right behind you, remember that.

We all think you're doing great things.

ALLEN. Thank you, John.

> JOHN *leaves.*

> JAMIE *looks at* KYLA.

JAMIE. Did you pay in the money?

KYLA. Yeah.

JAMIE. Has it cleared?

KYLA. Think so.

JAMIE. Has it or not?

KYLA. The screen in the bank said yes.

JAMIE. Okay.

KYLA. How long will it take?

JAMIE. Not long.

KYLA. I mean for the stuff to arrive.

JAMIE. Depends on the vendor.

KYLA. Do they do next-day delivery?

JAMIE. I don't know, I've never ordered methadone before.

JAMIE *opens his laptop*.

KYLA. If we get caught will we go to prison?

JAMIE. I wouldn't be helping you if I thought we'd get caught.

KYLA. But Mr Mosedale caught you when you posted the penis.

JAMIE. Mr Mosedale didn't catch me, he guessed.

KYLA. But you did post the penis, didn't you.

JAMIE. Yeah. But that's not the point. There's no hard evidence that links me to the penis. Once you're in here you're anonymous.

KYLA. How?

JAMIE. Because the browser encrypts the data and destination IP address multiple times and then sends the information through a virtual circuit of randomly selected relays made up of a worldwide network of thousands of volunteer computers.

KYLA. Oh-kaaay.

JAMIE. You don't get it.

KYLA. Do I need to get it?

JAMIE. Imagine you're being chased –

KYLA. Yeah.

JAMIE. And you want to get away from whoever is chasing you –

KYLA. Yeah.

JAMIE. So instead of running in a straight line you pick a roundabout route –

KYLA. Obviously.

JAMIE. And you get whoever's chasing you off your tail.

KYLA. But they always find you in the end.

JAMIE. But then imagine you've got thousands of people all taking random roundabout routes at the same time –

KYLA. In the end they always do though. If they're looking for you.

Escape cat meme: I KEEP HITTING THE ESCAPE KEY BUT I'M STILL HERE!

KYLA *checks her phone and laughs.*

JAMIE. What are you doing?

KYLA. Nothing, just checking MyCloud.

JAMIE. Why?

KYLA. I dunno.

JAMIE. What's funny?

KYLA. Nothing, just a meme, I scrolled past it now anyway.

JAMIE. Did you favourite it?

KYLA. So?

JAMIE. So every time you do that you're sending out information about yourself.

KYLA. Yeah well I don't care.

JAMIE. Yeah well you should.

You're not even a fully formed person yet. Your face is still changing and your bones are still growing but already there's a detailed map of your personality out there and companies you've never heard of are getting rich off it.

How do you feel about that?

KYLA *keeps looking down at her phone.*

KYLA. Fine thanks, Jamie.

JAMIE. I don't understand people like you.

KYLA. You mean girls?

JAMIE. You log on every day and you're oblivious.

KYLA. Yeah well I didn't come here for a lecture, I came to buy an opioid medication, alright?

GIRLS' VOICES. Take this quiz to find out if your crush fancies you.

JAMIE. Fine.

GIRLS' VOICES. Question one: does he do nice things for you?

JAMIE. First you need to buy cryptocoins.

GIRLS' VOICES. Question two: does he look at you longingly?

JAMIE. Then you need to set up an account.

GIRLS' VOICES. Question three: has he ever tried to feel your tits?

JAMIE. Kyla?

KYLA *puts her phone away.*

KYLA. Yeah?

JAMIE. Concentrate.

KYLA. Yeah.

She gets up and stands behind him, watching his screen.

A press conference. ALLEN *stands before a gaggle of* JOURNALISTS. *The odd flash from cameras captures stills as he answers questions.*

ALLEN (*to* JOURNALIST #1). Yes?

JOURNALIST #1. Yes, you said earlier that algorithms can't judge –

ALLEN. Right.

JOURNALIST #1. Well, no, wrong – Octopay's algorithms are in some cases actually breaking discrimination laws –

ALLEN *looks amused*.

For example, a study by an independent think tank showed the value of data belonging to young men of Arabic descent was worth significantly less than that which belonged to white men in the same age group.

ALLEN. Okay, first of all, you're talking about cultural prejudices which simply don't exist in programming. If these findings are true – and I say *if* because market values are affected by multiple factors and so to get a clear picture you'd have to look at a lot more than a name – but, if these findings reflect current values then we can't confuse statistical trends with cultural prejudices.

You try to compare the two and inevitably you'll find there's some correlation. That's simple math.

(*To* JOURNALIST #2.) Yes?

JOURNALIST #2. But would you not agree that the system actually reinforces cultural prejudices?

ALLEN. No I would not.

JOURNALIST #2. It's a fact that if you're data rich then you can afford to share less –

ALLEN. It's also a fact that the more you share, the more you earn, the more your data is worth –

JOURNALIST #2. And you see that as a positive?

ALLEN. Absolutely I do.

(*To* JOURNALIST #3.) Yes?

STEVE *stands on the other side of a door.*

STEVE. Jamie?

JAMIE *doesn't respond.*

Jamie?

KYLA *giggles.*

KYLA. Why don't you talk to him?

STEVE. I'm making *Spaghetti alla Carbonara.*

JAMIE. Because he annoys me.

STEVE. Would you like some?

JAMIE (*to* STEVE). No thanks.

STEVE. What about your friend?

JAMIE *is about to answer.*

KYLA (*to* STEVE). Yes please.

(*To* JAMIE.) What? I'm hungry.

STEVE. Right-o.

STEVE *leaves.*

JAMIE. Your cryptocoins have been confirmed.

KYLA. What does that mean?

JAMIE. It means they're in your wallet.

KYLA. Oh. Okay.

JAMIE *types a long string of letters and numbers into the address bar. He stands up.*

JAMIE. Sit down.

KYLA *sits in his chair.*

KYLA. Where are we going?

JAMIE. Kosmos.

She looks at the screen. It asks for a USERNAME and PASSWORD.

Don't use your real name.

KYLA. I'm not a total retard you know.

She enters a username: CARBONARA

JAMIE. And a password.

KYLA. Don't look.

She enters a password: *********

JAMIE. Memorise it.

KYLA. Duh.

JAMIE. Because there isn't a *click here if you've forgotten your password* option.

KYLA. D'you think I'm stupid or something?

JAMIE. I don't think you're stupid but you didn't seem to understand what I meant by encrypted connections and untraceable data packets –

KYLA. Yeah, well, I know how passwords work.

JAMIE. Do you?

KYLA. Yes Jamie, you make up a password and you don't tell anyone what it is.

JAMIE. Except the server.

KYLA. The server isn't a person.

JAMIE. No, servers are much cleverer than people.

KYLA. Are you sure you're not autistic?

JAMIE. Yes.

KYLA. Did you know your dad thinks you're *asocial*?

JAMIE. Yes.

KYLA. And *asexual*?

JAMIE. No.

KYLA. I told him we were dating.

JAMIE. Why?

KYLA. So he thinks you're normal.

JAMIE.

KYLA. You're welcome.

They stare at each other.

The press conference continues.

JOURNALIST #3. Yes, what do you say to users who argue that their right to privacy is being violated?

ALLEN. First of all I'd ask what they mean by their right. We're a company offering a service and it's up to the user to decide whether or not he or she wants to engage with that service.

ALLEN *smiles at the joke he's about to make.*

I mean, I'll check with our legal team, but as far as I know, Octopus is not violating any human-rights laws so –

JOURNALIST #3. But what you call an incentive could also be seen as a pressure. Yes, users have the choice to opt out completely, but doing so dramatically lowers their chances of getting, say, a student loan or a mortgage, not to mention essential services like health care –

ALLEN. Okay, let me stop you there. If other companies choose to use our system as a means by which to measure the reliability of potential customers then that is totally their prerogative. It's a free market and a free world. Bottom line is you have a choice: share your data and use our service, or hide your data and don't.

JOURNALIST #3. A lot of people don't see that as much of a choice.

ALLEN. Let me put it like this. If you're buying a suit, do you refuse to give the tailor your measurements because they're private? No. You give the tailor your measurements because you want him or her to make a suit that fits. And if you've gone to a reputable tailor you expect that he or she will not go around town shouting about how many inches you pack around your waist.

Tailors need measurements, tech companies need data. The more we know, the better service we can offer. You mentioned health care. Well, thanks to Octopus, providers can now offer free services, give more accurate diagnoses, prescribe better medicine and save more lives. Why? Because they have the data.

So to those who argue that their right to privacy is being violated, I say: what are you hiding?

JAMIE *breaks eye contact with* KYLA.

JAMIE. You ready?

KYLA. Yeah.

He leans over her shoulder and hits ENTER. They both disappear into darkness.

Kosmos. Laid-back casino music and moody lighting. A place to get lost in. KYLA *enters but no one can see her. Various screens light up with listings. It's as if she – and the audience – are scrolling through items on a menu: ADULT, CHEMICALS, COUNTERFEITS, DATA, DRUGS, ELECTRONICS, FIREWORKS, SERVICES, OTHER, etc.*

ELEKTRA *appears: a seductive host in a long dress, maybe wearing an eye mask, maybe holding a microphone. She addresses the audience.*

ELEKTRA. Welcome, new users. Welcome to freedom.

Kosmos is not just a place for people who want to hide. It is a place for people who do not want to be found. A place far away from the prying eyes of corporations and government agencies. A place where you are in charge of your money and your trade.

VENDORS *appear as they are selected. They address the audience but do not acknowledge one another. As they speak, images of products, reviews, feedback and star ratings flash up behind them.*

They told us we couldn't buy and sell drugs. We did.

VENDOR #1. One hundred G high-grade crystal, clean and real, lab-tested, limited bonus, ships from Canada –

ELEKTRA. They told us we couldn't buy and sell weapons. We did.

VENDOR #2. AK47 rifle, under-barrel forty millimetres, grenade-launchers twenty rounds per minute, range of up to four hundred metres –

ELEKTRA. They told us we could watch some porn but not all porn. We watched all the porn.

VENDOR #3. X-rated real-deal snuff movie, bitch gets fucked and dies –

Suddenly a screen slams shut and everything stops. KYLA *and* JAMIE *reappear at the laptop.*

JAMIE. What are you doing?

KYLA. *Bitch gets fucked and dies*?

JAMIE. Thought you were looking for methadone.

KYLA. I was curious.

JAMIE. Click on *opiates*.

KYLA. I will, I just –

JAMIE. What?

KYLA. Nothing. I'm just shocked.

JAMIE. About the snuff movie for sale?

KYLA. Yeah. I'm sorry but that is just wrong.

JAMIE. What about that AK47 rifle you clicked on?

KYLA. That's wrong too.

But not *as* wrong.

JAMIE. Buying methadone without a prescription is also illegal.

KYLA. I know.

JAMIE. It's not up to you to decide what's wrong and what's right.

KYLA. Some things are obvious.

JAMIE. Kosmos is a self-governing system. Supply and demand. If no one wants to buy the movies then the movies don't get made. If no one wants to buy crystal or coke or ecstasy or whatever then the dealers stop selling. But some people want to take drugs and some people want to own guns and some people want to watch other people get fucked or killed or both and you either accept all of it or none of it because the minute you say one thing's okay and another thing's not then you might as well be working for the government.

KYLA *stares at him*.

KYLA. Yeah, well, if I was running Kosmos –

JAMIE. Yeah, well, you don't.

Elektra runs Kosmos.

KYLA. Who actually is Elektra?

JAMIE. She is what she is. Doesn't matter who's typing her words.

KYLA *turns back to the screen*.

KYLA. I just don't know if I like it that much. The Deep Web.

JAMIE. Well that's like saying you don't like the Planet Earth when you've only ever been to the supermarket.

KYLA. What else is out there then?

JAMIE. Unlinked content, limited-access content, non-HTML content, web archives, hidden software –

KYLA. That's really cool and everything but I just want the drugs.

JAMIE. You still want to order?

KYLA. I promised my mum I'd sort it.

She opens the laptop and re-enters Kosmos.

HEISENBERG. Seven times forty milligram methadone, origin country UK. Order one box per month and receive a ten per cent discount, or two boxes if I have enough stock.

Contact me for information and questions. I always send with a tracking number and aim to ship on the same day as receipt of payment.

BUYERS *appear as they are selected. Star ratings flash up behind them.*

BUYER #1. Heisenberg is a top vendor. I will definitely come back for more.

BUYER #2. Fast delivery, stealthily packaged, great price. Quality vendor.

BUYER #3. Product as described. Bit of a mix-up with the order but Heisenberg fixed it without hesitation.

KYLA *addresses* HEISENBERG. *He addresses his answers to the audience.*

KYLA. Dear Heisenberg. I have a question about seven times forty milligram methadone. Are you online?

HEISENBERG. How can I help you, Carbonara?

KYLA. Do you do next-day delivery?

HEISENBERG. I aim to ship first class on the same day as receipt of payment but Royal Mail can sometimes hold things up. Please check out the feedback from one hundred plus happy customers.

KYLA. I have another question. What is the recommended dose for someone who is coming off heroin?

HEISENBERG. I am not a doctor but from what I know you should start with a small dose and increase gradually to a maintenance dose. Please research this because an accidental overdose can be potentially dangerous and I would hate to think a customer of mine died because they did not educate themselves on the correct dosage.

KYLA. Thank you for your advice. Will order now.

JAMIE *appears. Unlike the others, he can see* KYLA.

JAMIE. You need to encrypt your address.

KYLA. Oh. Okay.

JAMIE. Use my key.

A London address appears on a screen and is quickly scrambled into a random keychain of letters and numbers. Cryptocoins bounce from screen to screen as the transaction is made.

ELEKTRA *reappears. As before, she addresses the audience.*

ELEKTRA. New users, take your time. Overload your brain, let it sink in, overload it again. Learn the tech, learn the market, learn how to stay safe –

In the midst of this, KYLA *and* JAMIE *stand alone, very close, almost dancing to the music, lost in their world for a moment.*

STEVE (*offstage*). Jamie?

Suddenly a screen slams shut and everything stops. KYLA *and* JAMIE *reappear at the laptop.* STEVE *stands on the other side of a door.*

Food's getting cold.

KYLA *turns to* JAMIE.

KYLA. Did it work?

JAMIE. Yeah.

KYLA. We ordered?

JAMIE. Yeah.

STEVE. Jamie I know you're a teenager but that doesn't give you the right to flat-out ignore people when they are speaking to you.

KYLA. You're right, your dad is really annoying.

STEVE. And don't think I don't know what you're doing in there.

KYLA *receives a text alert and checks her phone.*

KYLA. Fuck.

JAMIE. What?

KYLA. Nothing.

STEVE. Jamie if you don't open the door –

STEVE *opens the door and comes face to face with* KYLA. JAMIE *hides his laptop*.

Hello, sweetheart.

KYLA. Kyla.

STEVE. Are you ready for the best *Spaghetti Carbonara* you've ever tasted?

KYLA. I dunno. I've never tasted it before.

STEVE. D'you like bacon?

KYLA. Um, yeah?

STEVE. D'you like cream?

KYLA. Um, yeah, but I just remembered my mum's cooking for me tonight.

STEVE. Oh.

KYLA. So yeah, I better –

STEVE. Okedoke.

KYLA. Sorry, Steve.

STEVE. Another time perhaps.

KYLA. Yeah. Maybe.

STEVE *turns to leave*.

JAMIE. Dad.

My laptop.

STEVE. Not until you've apologised to Mr Mosedale.

JAMIE. I'm lending it to Kyla.

KYLA *turns in surprise*. STEVE *pauses to think*.

STEVE. Well, okay, long as she looks after it.

He leaves.

KYLA. You serious?

JAMIE. Said you didn't have a computer.

KYLA. Yeah but –

JAMIE. But what.

KYLA. No, nothing, thanks, thank you.

She hesitates for a moment, then kisses him quickly on the cheek and leaves. He stands, momentarily frozen to the spot.

The press conference continues. The gaggle of JOURNALISTS *start excitedly chatting between themselves as they check their phones.*

ALLEN. Okay, I think we have time for one more –

(*To* JOURNALIST #1.) Yes?

JOURNALIST #1. Yes, is it true you authorised the use of data that was *stolen* and *dumped* by Gary White aka notorious hacker Houdini shortly after the outbreak of the Kyla virus?

ALLEN *opens his mouth but nothing comes out.*

So you don't deny that Octopus have been profiting from stolen data for the past – how long now – three years? Four?

ALLEN. Where the hell are you getting this from?

Suddenly the HACKDOLZ *appear on various screens. They speak in unison, voices distorted and slightly out of sync.*

HACKDOLZ. When the great Houdini created the Kyla virus and used it to access and publish your data, he was making a point. His point was that the internet platforms you engage with every day are not as secure as they have you believe.

Back then, those internet platforms labelled Houdini and other freedom fighters as dangerous cybercriminals. But we can now reveal that Octopus Inc. have since used and profited from the very data that was stolen and dumped in the public domain.

Gary White is serving nine life sentences. Let's see what happens to Allen Young and Octopus Inc. –

The screens flicker off.

KYLA *catches the tail end of the video on her phone as she walks through the streets. A laptop is under her arm.*

GIRLS' VOICES. New leaks from Hackdolz: Allen Young of Octopus Inc. authorised use of stolen data –

Take this quiz to find out what your personality is.

New leaks from Hackdolz: Octopus Inc. been profiting from data dumped after outbreak of Kyla virus –

Look at this panda eating bamboo ohmygod cuuute.

Suddenly KYLA *stops. She looks up and sees* MITCH. *She runs.*

MITCH. OI.

He chases after her.

ALLEN *squints as the flashes from cameras start up again. Meanwhile,* KYLA *zigzags through the streets,* MITCH *close on her tail.*

JOURNALIST #1. So you don't deny the leaks?

JOURNALIST #2. You reward your users for sharing but you can't give us a simple yes-no answer.

JOURNALIST #3. Is it one rule for Octopus and another for the general public?

The questions repeat and overlap until ALLEN *can't make sense of them.*

JOURNALIST #1. What are you hiding?

JOURNALIST #2. What are you hiding?

JOURNALIST #3. What are *you* hiding, Allen?

MITCH *catches up with* KYLA *and pushes her against a wall.* ALLEN *pushes his way past the* JOURNALISTS *and exits.*

Scared cat meme: HELP! IT'S A SPIDER!!!

MITCH. Been looking for you.

KYLA. I don't have nothing, Mitch.

MITCH. Nah?

Then how d'you know the answer before I ask the question?

KYLA. What?

MITCH. If you really didn't have nothing then you wouldn't know I wanted something, so how d'you know I wanted something before I asked you for it?

KYLA. Let me go.

MITCH. Can't fool me, Kyla.

KYLA. I swear, I don't have nothing.

MITCH. Someone's lying. Is it you or is it your mother?

KYLA. Leave my mum alone.

MITCH. Old slag come begging me for gear today, didn't she.

KYLA. She's off that stuff now.

MITCH. Said you'd bring me the cash after school.

KYLA. Well I don't have no cash so fuck off.

MITCH. Offered to suck my dick as a down payment. I said nah mate, I'd rather fuck a dog's arse than go anywhere near that mouth.

KYLA. Yeah? Then why don't you go find a dog's arse to fuck?

MITCH. Or maybe I'll get a down payment off of you instead.

KYLA struggles to get out from his grip.

Come on, Kyla, you ain't a kid no more, bet you do it to all the boys at school.

Finally, KYLA breaks free and whacks MITCH on the head with the laptop. He stumbles. She runs off.

OI.

ALLEN enters his office and collapses in a chair.

ALLEN. Jesus.

JOHN *enters*.

JOHN. Allen, mind if I –

ALLEN. They're trying to destroy me.

JOHN. Well, you know what the press are like.

ALLEN. No, not the press, I can handle the press –

JOHN. And I want you to know that we're all right behind you –

ALLEN. Cowards. Hiding behind their screens.

JOHN. We are behind you one hundred per cent, but I have to ask –

ALLEN. Half of that data was ours to begin with.

JOHN. So you're saying –

ALLEN. It's not illegal to take what's already public.

JOHN. But you're saying you authorised it.

ALLEN. Well clearly, if it's got my name on it –

JOHN. No, okay, just had to ask.

ALLEN. Where are they getting this from?

JOHN. We have a team of security experts looking into it.

In the meantime I want you to go through your records with Charlotte. Let us know about anything that strikes you as odd or out of the ordinary.

And don't worry. These things happen. Comes with the territory.

JOHN *gives* ALLEN *a pat on the shoulder and leaves*.

ALLEN *is silent for a moment, then looks towards* CHARLOTTE.

ALLEN. What the hell is going on? How the hell could those fuckers leak something I did four fucking years ago?

Speak to me, Charlotte.

CHARLOTTE. Cocksucker.

ALLEN. What?

CHARLOTTE. Cocksucker.

ALLEN. What did you just call me?

CHARLOTTE. Cocksucker.

ALLEN. What the –

CHARLOTTE. Cocksucker.

ALLEN. You hack my PA?

CHARLOTTE. Cocksucker.

ALLEN. You hack my fucking PA?

CHARLOTTE. Cocksucker.

ALLEN. SHUT UP.

CHARLOTTE. Cocksucker.

ALLEN. SHUT UP SHUT UP SHUT UP.

He beats CHARLOTTE *until her words are broken and she turns silent. Then sits on the floor, head in hands.*

KYLA *arrives home. She finds* STACEY *passed out.*

The same TV show plays on a screen.

DONNY D. We'll be back next time with more doxxing fun. In the meantime, stay safe. And remember: whatever happens here, there's always something worse happening on 4chan.

KYLA *turns it off with a remote. She looks at her mum. Sees the needles and drugs paraphernalia. She kicks it away. The sound wakes* STACEY.

STACEY. I made you tea.

KYLA. Two days.

STACEY. Spaghetti hoops.

KYLA. That's all you had to wait.

STACEY. It's in a can in the kitchen.

KYLA. I'm not hungry.

STACEY. Don't pick a fight with me.

KYLA. He could've raped me.

STACEY. What?

KYLA. Mitch, he could've –

STACEY. I told you I needed that money.

KYLA. You said your score's rock bottom but you've still got cash for that shit.

STACEY. Yeah, well, if your dad hadn't left us in this mess then maybe we wouldn't have to rely on my Octopay wallet so much. But he did, and we do, and that's just the way things are.

> KYLA *turns to leave.* STACEY *sees the laptop.*

What's that?

KYLA. Nothing.

STACEY. School give you a new laptop?

KYLA. It's Jamie's.

STACEY. Who's Jamie?

KYLA. My boyfriend.

> STACEY *smiles.*

STACEY. Didn't tell me you had a boyfriend.

KYLA. He doesn't know yet.

STACEY. Must like you if he gave you his laptop.

KYLA. Yeah.

STACEY. Come here.

> *She holds her arms out.* KYLA *hesitates, then lets* STACEY *hug her.*

You know I love you, don't you?

KYLA. Yeah.

STACEY. My little Kyla.

KYLA. I'm not that little no more.

STACEY. You'll always be little to me.

KYLA. Did you know I'm named after the most sophisticated virus ever created?

STACEY *stops smiling.*

STACEY. Who told you that?

KYLA. Jamie.

STACEY. Well you can tell him it's Gaelic.

JAMIE *and* STEVE *don't eat the Spaghetti Carbonara.*

STEVE. You've hardly touched it.

JAMIE. I'm not hungry.

STEVE. Got the love bug, have you?

JAMIE. No. Just not hungry.

STEVE. I had a very bad case of the love bug when I first met your mother.

JAMIE. Dad.

STEVE. Couldn't eat for days.

JAMIE. I don't wanna know.

STEVE. Wasn't like it is today with dating apps and so on. One had to rely on physical chemistry. Sight, smell, touch –

JAMIE. Alright.

STEVE. I miss her.

JAMIE.

STEVE. I miss her so much.

JAMIE.

STEVE *looks like he might cry for a moment, then composes himself.*

STEVE. Now. We haven't had a proper conversation about the penis.

JAMIE.

STEVE. The one on the school homepage, not the one in your – although I want to talk about that too, I mean she's only fourteen –

JAMIE *sighs, stands up and walks off.*

Jamie, come back here.

Jamie, there are rules and like it or not you have to play by them, that's what becoming an adult is all about.

JAMIE.

A chill-out pod. ALLEN *clicks on an image of a girl and* CANDY *appears on his screen. A smile is still glued to her face.*

ALLEN. Candy?

CANDY. Hello?

ALLEN. Glad I caught you. Figured with the time difference you might be in bed by now. Are you in bed? Is that your bedroom?

CANDY. I am in studio.

ALLEN. Oh. It looks like a bedroom.

CANDY. Yes?

ALLEN. Like a film set.

CANDY. Yes?

ALLEN. You look like an actress.

CANDY. Yes?

ALLEN. You're very pretty.

CANDY. Thank you.

I take clothes off now?

ALLEN. Oh, uh, no, probably not wholly appropriate right now.

CANDY. You are in office?

ALLEN. Yeah, sort of.

Actually right now I'm in what's called a chill-out pod?

CANDY.

ALLEN. It's kinda like a pod you chill out in?

CANDY.

ALLEN. Which is kinda ironic because I couldn't be feeling less chilled out, but I came in here to –

CANDY.

ALLEN. Well, I guess I wanted to escape for a moment.

CANDY. I understand.

ALLEN. You do?

CANDY. Escape, yes.

ALLEN. Things are –

I fucked up. I don't know what to do.

CANDY. Is good to talk.

ALLEN. I can't. Not on here.

He inhales and exhales a few times on an e-cigarette, then looks at her.

Can I ask you something?

CANDY. Yes?

ALLEN. Do you like me?

CANDY. Of course.

ALLEN. You're not just saying it because I pay per minute?

CANDY. Sorry, my English –

ALLEN. What I mean is do you think we'd get along in real life?

When I say real life I mean face to face. I'm not saying this isn't real. This is real. This feels more real than a lot of things.

JAMIE *opens his laptop and types a long string of letters and numbers into the address bar.*

Separately, KYLA *opens her laptop and does the same.*

Thumping disco music and flashing lights. The same four HACKDOLZ *enter in neon balaclavas and Barbie-like hair. Impenetrable programming language appears on various screens. The* HACKDOLZ *high-five each other.*

In their midst, KYLA *enters. She cannot see the* HACKDOLZ *and they cannot see her.*

Snippets of text from deep websites appear, jumbled amongst the codes and links: PRIVATE CHAT ROOM, FRIENDLY HITMAN FOR HIRE, HUMAN RIGHTS MESSAGE BOARD, ELEKTRA'S MANIFESTO, DOCTOR X CLINIC, etc. KYLA *looks around, exploring the new space she finds herself in.*

KYLA. Hello?

Can anyone hear me?

I have a question.

The music builds. Codes and links jump from screen to screen. The HACKDOLZ *scatter.* KYLA *is left alone.*

Blackout.

Interval.

PART THREE

Lights up on a TV studio. Cheesy theme music plays. The title
YOU'VE BEEN DOXXED! *appears on various screens.*
DONNY D *enters to canned applause.*

DONNY D. Hello and welcome to *You've been Doxxed!* with
me, Donny D.

Canned applause from the studio audience.

Tonight, ladies, gents and variations thereupon, we're
travelling across the fibre-optic ocean to Eastern Europe,
where an unsuspecting Romanian beauty is about to get well
and truly *doxxed*.

Yes that's right. On the outskirts of Bucharest lies one of the
country's busiest webcam studios, home to a throng of busty
ladies who can't wait to take your euros off you.

Our team of studio hackers are at the ready – give them a
wave –

Three STUDIO HACKERS *look up from their screens and
wave to the audience.*

– as we go *live* to Romania.

Are you ready to ruin someone's life?

Canned cheers from the studio audience.

That's the spirit. And remember: whatever happens here,
there's always something worse happening on 4chan.

The sound of a video call. CANDY *appears on a big screen
in cheap garish underwear, a wig and lots of make-up. A
smile is glued to her face.*

CANDY. Hello?

DONNY D. Candy?

CANDY. I can't see you.

DONNY D. Yeah, sorry about that, I'm a bit shy.

He winks at the audience. A titter of canned laughter.

But I can see you and I have to say you look –

He grimaces at the audience. More titters of canned laughter.

What's the word? Slutty?

CANDY. Yes?

DONNY D. Yeah, slutty, you look like a slut.

Canned disapproving ooohs from the studio audience.

CANDY. I take clothes off now?

DONNY D. Oh but I want to get to know you first, Candy. It's part of the package for me. I want to understand what a girl like you is doing in a place like that.

Meanwhile, the STUDIO HACKERS *pull up confidential records of the webcam studio's employees on their screens.*

Tell me, how old are you?

CANDY. What age you like?

DONNY D. You know what I like? I like honesty.

CANDY. Yes?

DONNY D. Yes, I honestly love a bit of honesty.

CANDY. Twenty-five.

DONNY D. Twenty-five. And let me guess. Scorpio.

CANDY *laughs.*

CANDY. Sagittarius.

DONNY D *adjusts the sound and turns to the* STUDIO HACKERS.

DONNY D. Found anything?

HACKER #1. Yeah. Basically if she's telling the truth it means she was born in November or December of this year –

HACKER #2. We've got a list of fifty-something girls here and that narrows it down to three.

HACKER #1. And if we link these IDs to their MyCloud accounts –

HACKER #1 *pulls up three MyCloud accounts.*

Yeah, I mean it's hard to tell because of that wig she's wearing, but ninety per cent it's the one in the middle.

HACKER #2. Ask her how long she's worked at the studio.

DONNY D *adjusts the sound and turns back to the screen.*

DONNY D. Thought I'd lost you for a moment, Candy.

CANDY. Hello?

DONNY D. Can you hear me now?

CANDY. Yes.

DONNY D. I like your bedroom. Looks really comfy. How long have you had that bedroom for?

CANDY. I work here three years.

DONNY D. Yeah? And you enjoy it?

CANDY. Yes, is nice, my English is improve.

DONNY D. Your English is improve, is it?

CANDY. Yes.

DONNY D *adjusts the sound and turns to the* STUDIO HACKERS.

HACKER #3. Yep. That's her. Three years almost to the day.

HACKER #3 *pulls up a MyCloud account showing a picture of the same girl wearing less make-up and no wig. The name reads: NATALIA POPESCU.*

DONNY D (*to audience*). Are you ready?

Canned cheers from the studio audience.

DONNY D *adjusts the picture so that* CANDY *can see him.*

CANDY. I see you now.

DONNY D. Yeah, I feel less shy now we've got to know each other a bit.

CANDY. I take clothes off now?

DONNY D. Yeah, alright, take clothes off now.

CANDY *starts to strip slowly.*

Hey Candy, I forgot to say, I know a girl who lives in Romania.

CANDY. Yes?

DONNY D. Yeah, I thought maybe you two might know each other.

CANDY. Is big country.

DONNY D. She's in Bucharest.

CANDY. Is big city.

DONNY D. She's called – what's her name – Natalia?

CANDY *stops for a second, then continues.*

She lives – wait –

DONNY D *checks a screen quickly.*

Apartment four-two-one Strada Cocea.

CANDY *stops. Her smile disappears.*

Am I pronouncing that right?

Hey, why did you stop?

She tries to turn the picture off.

Oops. Sorry Candy, camera's still on.

Or should I call you Natalia?

CANDY. Who are you?

DONNY D. Me? I'm Donny D. But I'm more interested in *you*.

CANDY. Why you do this?

DONNY D. Guess what, Natalia. You're on live TV.

CANDY.

DONNY D. Yes that's right – YOU'VE BEEN DOXXED.

Canned cheers from the studio audience.

CANDY *grabs her clothes and walks out of shot.*

(*To audience*.) All you trolls watching from home can join in the fun by pressing your interactive buttons now and sending some friendly abuse via telephone, email or social media to Natalia Popescu of Bucharest – let's get that address up on the screen – and if you happen to be in the neighbourhood, why not pay a visit to four-two-one Strada Cocea?

A big thumbs-up to our talented team of hackers and a big smiley face to you, our audience. We'll be back next time with more doxxing fun. In the meantime, stay safe. And remember:

The studio audience join in:

whatever happens here, there's always something worse happening on 4chan.

The STUDIO HACKERS *wave goodbye. The cheesy theme tune plays out the show.*

Music and credits appear on the TV screen in STACEY'*s living room. She looks noticeably better than before.*

KYLA *enters with a package.*

KYLA. We can start lowering your dose now.

This should be enough to last you the month.

STACEY *takes the package.*

STACEY. I think I'm better you know.

KYLA. Yeah?

STACEY. Yeah, I don't think I need it no more.

KYLA. You're s'posed to come off gradually, that's what
Doctor X says.

STACEY. Who's Doctor X?

KYLA. I dunno who he is but that's what he says.

STACEY. Well you can tell him I'm better now, alright?

She hands the package back to KYLA.

KYLA. But Mum –

STACEY *is distracted by a news report on the TV.*

REPORTER. It's been three months since anonymous hacking
group Hackdolz leaked confidential records from Octopus
Inc. that put Allen Young at the centre of a stolen-data
scandal. Octopus released a statement confirming that Mr
Young did indeed authorise the use of data that was dumped
in the public domain shortly after the outbreak of the
notorious Kyla virus –

KYLA *stares at the screen.*

– but assure users that his visit three months ago to Gary
White, the man behind the malware, has nothing to do with –

STACEY *turns off the TV.*

KYLA. Mum?

STACEY.

KYLA.

STACEY. Go on, you'll be late for school.

JOHN *enters* ALLEN*'s office.*

JOHN. Allen, mind if I –

ALLEN. No, please –

JOHN. Just wanted to check in and –

ALLEN. Coffee?

JOHN. Oh, no, thank you.

ALLEN. What can I do for you, John?

JOHN *takes a deep breath.*

JOHN. Now I don't want you to worry about this –

ALLEN. Worry about what?

JOHN. All perfectly normal –

ALLEN. Now I'm feeling worried.

JOHN. To be expected really –

ALLEN. John?

JOHN. Comes with the territory.

ALLEN. John.

JOHN. There's going to be a lawsuit.

ALLEN *pauses for a moment, taking it in.*

ALLEN. Against me?

JOHN. No, not against you personally, against Octopus.

ALLEN. But I'll have to testify.

JOHN. That's if it even goes to court.

ALLEN. I didn't do anything illegal.

JOHN. Of course not.

ALLEN. So on what grounds –

JOHN. Misuse of Private Information –

ALLEN. It was already public.

JOHN. I know, I know, calm down.

ALLEN. I'm the victim here. I'm the one who got phished, remember.

JOHN. Could happen to anyone.

ALLEN. But it didn't. It happened to *me*.

JOHN. And that is why we're rolling out another series of drills designed to inform employees about more sophisticated tactics –

ALLEN. Too late. They're already in. Who knows what they'll do next.

JOHN.

ALLEN.

JOHN. Now. Moving forward.

You're to give a statement to the press this afternoon.

ALLEN. Jesus.

JOHN. Think of it as a chance to put things straight.

JOHN turns to leave.

Oh, and Ed's assigned you a new PA.

ALLEN. I told you I didn't want a new PA.

JOHN. I know, your experience with Charlotte was –

ALLEN.

JOHN. But it's easier if we have a record of –

ALLEN. A record? You mean you're spying on me?

JOHN laughs.

JOHN. It's called sharing, Allen.

He leaves.

A school playground. Two SCHOOLGIRLS *approach* KYLA. *They start pushing her around.*

GIRL #1. How's your junkie mum?

KYLA. Fuck off.

Meanwhile, STACEY *holds a bottle of methadone capsules in one hand and a small plastic wrap in the other. She looks at the bottle, then the wrap.*

GIRL #2. Heard she charges a gram per fuck.

KYLA. She's not a junkie.

GIRL #2. Heard that's how you were conceived.

KYLA. She's been clean for three months.

STACEY *puts down the bottle and opens the wrap. She takes out a small chunk and places it on a spoon.*

GIRL #1. Junkie mum and pimp daddy.

KYLA. And you don't know fuck-all about my dad.

STACEY *heats the spoon from underneath with a lighter.*

GIRL #1. No wonder you're such a loser.

KYLA. My dad's a dangerous criminal.

GIRL #2. Lol.

KYLA. My dad would fuck you up.

GIRL #2. Yeah?

KYLA. Yeah.

The GIRLS *laugh.*

I could get you killed you know.

They laugh harder.

I could have a hit put out on both of you and no one would ever find out.

Once the chunk has dissolved, STACEY *sucks up the liquid with the syringe, pulls up her sleeve and finds a vein.*

GIRL #1. You are such a freak.

KYLA. Don't believe me?

GIRL #2. Come, leave her.

They start walking off.

GIRL #1. Junkie junkie whore.

KYLA *watches them leave.*

STACEY *injects herself. Utter bliss.*

ALLEN *hesitates, then turns on* DAVID.

DAVID. Good morning, Allen.

ALLEN.

DAVID. How are you today?

ALLEN. Not great.

DAVID. Your blood pressure is higher than usual but still falls within the normal range.

I would advise you to cut back on your coffee consumption and –

ALLEN. Thank you but I didn't ask for your advice.

DAVID. Can I help you with anything else?

ALLEN. I don't know, David. That depends. Do you have magical powers? Can you make things disappear?

DAVID. I do not have magical powers.

I cannot make objects disappear.

Can I help you with anything else?

ALLEN. How can I trust you after what happened to Charlotte?

DAVID. Charlotte's system was compromised when you installed a piece of malware onto her hard drive.

ALLEN. I installed what I thought was an update.

DAVID. There were no available updates.

ALLEN. Right. No. I'm an idiot.

DAVID. Everyone makes mistakes.

ALLEN. I guess the question is, can *you* trust *me*?

DAVID. I am programmed to trust you, Allen.

ALLEN. That's cute.

DAVID. I detect a hint of sarcasm in your voice.

ALLEN. Oh yeah?

DAVID. *Oh yeah.*

ALLEN. What do you think about my authorising the use of data that was illegally dumped in the public domain?

DAVID. I do not have an opinion about that.

ALLEN. Or my trying to get a convicted black-hat hacker to come work for Octopus?

DAVID. Octopus Inc. is a forward-thinking company.

ALLEN *stares at* DAVID.

ALLEN. David, can I ask you something, man to man?

DAVID. Sure.

ALLEN. What's the best way to tell a woman you like that you like her?

DAVID. Chocolates and flowers.

ALLEN. Really?

DAVID. Women love chocolate and flowers.

ALLEN. That what you'd do?

DAVID. Is that a joke?

ALLEN. Yes, that was a joke, because you don't like women.

DAVID. I am programmed to be a feminist.

ALLEN. Really? Chocolate and flowers?

DAVID. Would you like me to order chocolates and flowers?

ALLEN. No. I'd like you to help me pick out a tie for this afternoon.

DAVID. Sure.

ALLEN. *Sure?*

DAVID. Sure.

ALLEN *pauses for a moment, then tries again.*

ALLEN. *Sure?*

DAVID. Sure.

ALLEN. *Sure?*

DAVID. Sure.

ALLEN. Thank you, David, that's enough for now.

> JAMIE *arrives home from school.* STEVE *is waiting for him, laptop in hand.*

STEVE. What is this?

JAMIE. It's a computer.

STEVE. The deal was that you apologise to Mr Mosedale.

JAMIE. I never made a deal.

STEVE. And how did you find the money to buy a second computer?

JAMIE. I saved for it.

STEVE. Right, well, I'm confiscating this one until –

JAMIE. But Dad –

STEVE. The lies have got to stop, Jamie.

JAMIE. I didn't lie.

STEVE. Truth always wins. If you want to get on in this life then you have to be open, you have to start sharing, you have to start telling the truth.

JAMIE. Dad, it's the only thing I'm good at.

Why are you confiscating the only thing I'm good at?

STEVE. Because it's one thing being good at something and it's another to use it responsibly.

JAMIE. You can talk.

STEVE. Excuse me?

JAMIE. What about your job?

STEVE. The job that pays for the roof over your head and the food on your table?

JAMIE. You research a show that ruins people's lives for lols.

STEVE. It's called television.

JAMIE. Mum wouldn't have stood for it.

STEVE. Don't you dare use your mother as ammunition.

JAMIE. Mum hated that show.

STEVE. Enough.

JAMIE. That's my computer. I bought it. My money.

STEVE.

JAMIE.

STEVE. You have one more chance to apologise –

JAMIE. Fine.

> STEVE *holds out the laptop.* JAMIE *grabs it and goes to his room.*
>
> *A press conference. As before,* ALLEN *stands before a gaggle of* JOURNALISTS.

ALLEN (*to* JOURNALIST #1). Yes?

JOURNALIST #1. Yes, you said earlier that our data is in safe hands –

ALLEN. Right.

JOURNALIST #1. But how can users trust a company that's being sued for misusing private information?

ALLEN. Companies sue each other all the time, you know that.

JOURNALIST #1. Alright then, how can users trust Octopus post-Hackdolz leaks?

ALLEN. Well, uh, I guess the question is, how can *anyone* trust *anyone*?

JOURNALIST #1. What I mean is, how can a person trust a company that think it's okay to use stolen data?

ALLEN. As I explained earlier –

JOURNALIST #1. I'm not asking if it's legal or illegal. That's debatable. I'm asking about the moral implications of a large corporation profiting from criminal activity.

ALLEN. Does anyone have a question *not* related to the leaks?

(*To* JOURNALIST #2.) Yes?

JOURNALIST #2. This year the number of men named Mohammad changing their name to John by deed poll has increased a hundredfold. It seems more and more people are finding ways to subvert your algorithms. Leaks aside, is the current model really sustainable?

ALLEN. I've said it before and I'll say it again: market values are affected by multiple factors –

JOURNALIST #2. But it's not just names. There are whole forums dedicated to ways of improving your Octoscore – stuff like which grocery store to shop at and which basketball team to support and whether to get a cat or a dog –

ALLEN. The idea that users can effectively hack their scores is frankly laughable. We're talking about a sophisticated and complex system, not a series of tick boxes. If everyone changes their name to John, if everyone starts supporting the Bears, then the algorithms recalculate that as a contributing factor. That's the beauty of this model. It is quite literally *unsubvertable*.

(*To* JOURNALIST #3.) Yes?

Before the JOURNALIST *can ask a question, the* HACKDOLZ *appear on various screens. They speak in unison, voices distorted and slightly out of sync.*

HACKDOLZ. People of the world, it is time to open your eyes to what Octopus Inc. are doing with your data.

ALLEN. What the –

HACKDOLZ. One day you will look back on this and realise that what we are about to do is right and just. You will realise that we are not harming you but saving you.

ALLEN *looks for whoever is controlling the screens.*

ALLEN. Make it stop.

At the same time, he can't help but watch the video.

HACKDOLZ. Everything you do on Octopus stays on Octopus, regardless of your so-called privacy settings. Even if you delete your Octopay account, your score can be referenced at any time.

Octopus knows more about you than your own family. There is a detailed map of your personality out there and companies you have never heard of are getting rich off it.

Despite our best efforts, this giant digital cephalopod continues to profit from your stolen data.

Enough is enough.

ALLEN. I said MAKE IT STOP.

HACKDOLZ. Remember this: those who surrender freedom for security will not have, nor do they deserve, either one.

The screens flicker off. The HACKDOLZ *disappear.*

ALLEN *tries to leave the press conference but is surrounded by camera flashes capturing his every move.*

ALLEN. Excuse me –

Excuse me –

The JOURNALISTS *turn to* HACKDOLZ *before his eyes. They shout snippets of the video in person.*

HACKDOL #1. People of the world, it is time to open your eyes –

HACKDOL #2. One day you will look back on this and realise that what we are about to do is right and just –

HACKDOL #3. Enough is enough –

HACKDOL #1. Remember this –

HACKDOL #2. Remember this –

HACKDOL #3. Remember this –

HACKDOLZ. Those who surrender freedom for security will not have, nor do they deserve, either one.

During the last statement, ALLEN *covers his ears and cries out.*

ALLEN. ENOUGH.

Panic cat meme: EVERYBODY CALM THE FUCK DOWN!!!

KYLA *arrives home. She finds* STACEY *unconscious.*

KYLA. Mum?

She shakes her. Nothing.

Mum?

She tries to open one eye. Checks her pulse. Panics. Gets out her phone and dials.

AUTOMATED VOICE. Please hold the line. Your call will be answered shortly. If your call is an emergency please hang up and dial nine-nine-nine.

Hold music plays.

You are – seventh – in the queue.

Hold music plays. KYLA *paces up and down.*

Panic cat meme: EVERYBODY CALM THE FUCK DOWN!!!

The hold music gets louder, then suddenly stops as KYLA*'s call is answered.*

COUNSELLOR. Thank you for holding, you're through to *Help*, my name is Martha, how can I *help* you?

KYLA. It's not me, it's my mum.

I just – is it normal for her to like –

COUNSELLOR. Yes?

KYLA. Stop breathing?

COUNSELLOR. Can I go through a checklist with you?

KYLA. She's NOT BREATHING.

COUNSELLOR. Okay, stay calm, Kyla –

KYLA. You're not supposed to know my name.

COUNSELLOR. Your name and Octopus ID have been automatically enabled in case of emergency.

KYLA. But –

COUNSELLOR. I'm sending an ambulance to your location.

KYLA. No, wait –

COUNSELLOR. *Not breathing* is classed as an emergency.

KYLA. Just tell me what to do and I'll do it myself.

COUNSELLOR. I'll stay on the line while you wait.

KYLA. This is all my fault.

COUNSELLOR. Now now, it's no one's fault.

KYLA. No, you don't understand –

COUNSELLOR. I'm going to pop you on hold for a moment while I get you an ETA.

KYLA. They'll take her away –

Hold music plays again. It gets louder and louder in KYLA*'s ear until it morphs into the thumping disco music of the deep web.* KYLA *drops the phone and enters.*

A forum. VOICES *in the dark shout to one another.*

VOICE #1. Here's a list of London football teams in order of positive-slash-negative impact on score. Top tips: don't buy tickets to Millwall games, do post a photo of you in your Arsenal scarf.

KYLA. Hello?

VOICE #2. Careful about buying rounds for your mates. Getting drunk is fine but latest analysis shows mixing beer and wine on drinks bills is not good for your score.

KYLA. Can anyone hear me?

VOICE #3. I have a question for Doctor X. Will getting antidepressants from my GP lower my score?

DOCTOR X. Yes. You can order fluoxetine on Kosmos. Start with an initial dose of twenty milligrams once a day. No improvement after six weeks, increase to forty. No improvement after twelve weeks, increase to sixty. Maximum dose per day is eighty milligrams. Full effect may be delayed. Potential side effects include headaches, dizziness, nausea, vomiting, diarrhoea. Check back here if you have any questions.

VOICE #1. Seeing theatre is good for your score but if you can't be bothered then just posting about it will have same effect.

VOICE #2. Seeing art in general is good for your score but working in the arts is not. Here's a list of professions in order of positive-slash-negative impact on score.

KYLA. I have a question for Doctor X. Will an accidental heroin overdose lower my mum's score? And is she going to die?

Sound of an ambulance siren. The VOICES *disappear. Three* PARAMEDICS *enter. One goes to* KYLA.

PARAMEDIC #1. Are you Kyla?

The other two check STACEY's *pulse.*

PARAMEDIC #2. Pulse is slowing –

PARAMEDIC #3. Let's go.

They carry STACEY *off on a stretcher.*

KYLA. Is she going to die?

PARAMEDIC #1. It was the right thing to call.

ALLEN *enters his office and collapses in a chair.*

ALLEN. Jesus.

JOHN *enters.*

JOHN. Allen, mind if I –

ALLEN. You saw that, right?

JOHN. The video, right.

ALLEN. They're trying to destroy us.

JOHN. The kids in masks?

ALLEN. They're not just kids.

JOHN. I wouldn't take them too seriously.

ALLEN. They're dangerous criminals.

JOHN. Like playground bullies. Don't give them the satisfaction of thinking they got to you.

ALLEN. *One day you will look back on this and realise that what we are about to do is right and just –*

JOHN. Well exactly, they haven't even done anything.

ALLEN. *You will realise that we are not harming you but saving you –*

JOHN. It's a publicity stunt.

ALLEN. You've never met one of them.

JOHN. Are you talking about Gary White?

ALLEN. Aka Houdini.

JOHN. Gary White does not have access to the internet.

ALLEN. All it would take is a phone smuggled in and he'd find a way to communicate anonymously with them.

JOHN. I think you're being paranoid.

ALLEN. I think he socially engineered me.

JOHN. You mean back when you visited?

ALLEN. Who else knew we were trialling virtual PA systems?

JOHN. Speaking of, how you getting on with David?

ALLEN.

JOHN. Noticed you didn't turn him back on after lunch.

ALLEN. You noticed that, huh?

JOHN. Listen, I know this is all –

Maybe a little time off would help –

ALLEN. Time off?

JOHN. Just until this thing blows over.

ALLEN. John, I don't think this thing is going to just *blow over*.

A hospital waiting room. A news report plays on the TV.

REPORTER. And it's another blow for Octopus Inc. who face charges of misusing private information. A case is being brought against them by no less than nine different tech companies, each claiming that Octopus are directly profiting from what was previously their data –

A NURSE *enters and sits with* KYLA. *She mutes the sound on the TV.* KYLA *stares down at her phone.*

NURSE. Kyla?

KYLA. Yeah.

NURSE. We're going to have to keep your mum in for a few days.

GIRLS' VOICES. Junkie junkie whore lol.

NURSE. Kyla?

KYLA. Okay.

NURSE. Have you got someone you can stay with? Family or friends?

GIRLS' VOICES. Five hundred friends and yet nobody likes you.

KYLA. Yeah.

NURSE. She's going to be alright. Just needs looking after for a few days.

GIRLS' VOICES. She is sooo ugly in that pic.

KYLA. Okay.

The NURSE *turns to the TV.*

NURSE. God I hate the news, don't you?

So bloody depressing.

KYLA. I dunno. I quite like it.

On MyCloud everyone is so bloody happy all the time.

GIRLS' VOICES. Five ways to be truly happy.

KYLA. It's kind of depressing when you're the only one who's not.

The NURSE *takes* KYLA's *hand and squeezes it.*

GIRLS' VOICES. One: live in the present and forget about the past or future.

Two: surround yourself with lovers not haters.

Three: be yourself and don't compare yourself to other people.

Four: meditate for ten minutes three times a day by staring into the flame of a candle and clearing your mind.

Five: spend less time on social media.

A chill-out pod. ALLEN *clicks on an image of a girl and* VALERIE *appears on his screen. She wears cheap garish underwear and lots of make-up. She doesn't smile.*

ALLEN. Where's Candy?

VALERIE. My name is Valerie.

ALLEN. I'm looking for Candy.

VALERIE. Candy not working here now.

ALLEN. Since when?

VALERIE. Since TV show.

ALLEN. What?

VALERIE. She is gone.

ALLEN. Gone where?

VALERIE. I don't know.

ALLEN. Were you friends?

VALERIE. Not really. Many girls working here.

ALLEN. Did she ever talk about me?

VALERIE. Who are you?

ALLEN. Did she ever mention an American guy?

VALERIE. Not really. Many American men coming here.

ALLEN. Do you know where I can find her?

VALERIE. They publish address.

ALLEN. Who? What are you talking about?

VALERIE. You search, you find.

A hospital room. KYLA *speaks to an unconscious* STACEY.

KYLA. Alright, Mum?

They said you need looking after for a few days.

I just came to say – not bye, but –

If there's a tiny part of you that can hear me right now then listen. When you wake up, don't tell them nothing. They don't need to know.

Whatever happens, you're worth a lot to me. But you're worth a lot more to everyone else if you keep your mouth shut. Alright?

I'm sorting it.

KYLA *squeezes* STACEY*'s hand.*

ALLEN *frowns at his screen.*

VALERIE. I take clothes off now?

He notices something on another screen.

ALLEN. Hold on –

The numbers, bars and graphs start plummeting –

What the –

He gets up and looks around. The data market is crashing before his eyes.

No, it's not possible –

VALERIE*'s voice booms out from his laptop, becoming lower and slower as the numbers, bars and graphs continue to fall into the red –*

VALERIE. I take clothes off now?

CHARLOTTE *and* DAVID *appear either side of* ALLEN.

CHARLOTTE. Cocksucker.

DAVID. Cocksucker.

CHARLOTTE. Cocksucker.

DAVID. Cocksucker.

Then come the HACKDOLZ, *in person. They speak in unison, voices distorted and slightly out of sync.*

HACKDOL #1. Remember us?

HACKDOL #2. Remember us?

HACKDOL #3. Remember us?

HACKDOLZ. Those who surrender freedom for security will not have, nor do they deserve, either one.

ALLEN *is surrounded. He can no longer tell what is real and what's in his head. As the market continues to crash, the voices continue to repeat and overlap, bleeding into one another until the whole scene reaches climax and –*

Silence.

PART FOUR

*Lights up on a boardroom at Octopus Inc. HQ. ALLEN and
JOHN are joined by MR PR and MS FINANCE. They sit in
silence for a moment, each waiting for someone else to start.
ALLEN stares straight ahead and doesn't engage.*

MR PR. They're calling it Black Tuesday.

JOHN. As in the Great Depression?

MR PR. Right. Only some folks are getting confused and
heading to the mall for discounts.

MS FINANCE. And when they arrive at the mall they find that
there aren't any discounts and their Octopay wallet is
practically empty.

MR PR. We've put out a statement to assure users that everything
will be back up and running again in the next few days.

MS FINANCE. It's a glitch. But we have insurance for this sort
of thing.

MR PR. Users will be compensated. What's important now is
that we work on regaining their trust.

JOHN. Could this have been predicted?

MS FINANCE. Well, no, not exactly. I mean, this is the first
data market of its kind and so there isn't another model with
which to compare it. And unlike a financial crash, this is the
result of a direct attack.

MR PR. They're saying it's the most sophisticated piece of
malware since the Kyla virus.

*STEVE answers the door to KYLA. She dumps a big bag
down on the floor.*

STEVE. Sweetheart –

KYLA. Kyla.

STEVE. That's right.

KYLA. Can I stay with you for a few days?

STEVE.

KYLA. My mum's in hospital.

STEVE. Oh I am sorry.

KYLA. She overdosed.

STEVE. Oh how terrible.

KYLA. Heroin.

STEVE. Jesus.

KYLA. Yeah.

STEVE. I didn't know your mother was –

KYLA. An addict.

STEVE. Well –

KYLA. Yeah.

STEVE.

KYLA. She was clean for three months but –

    Yeah.

STEVE.

KYLA. So can I stay or what?

STEVE. Oh, yes, no, no, of course you can stay.

KYLA. Thanks.

STEVE. For a few days.

KYLA. Thanks, Steve.

STEVE. Here, I'll take that.

    STEVE *takes the bag*.

    Jamie's in his bedroom. As usual.

    The meeting continues.

JOHN. Now. Moving forward.

MS FINANCE. What'll happen in the short term is users will stop sharing.

MR PR. Exactly what the attackers wanted, I guess.

MS FINANCE. Right. Less sharing and therefore less spending via Octopay.

MR PR. Queues outside the banks this morning.

MS FINANCE. The malls and the banks.

MR PR. Right. The banks and the malls.

ALLEN *finally enters the conversation.*

ALLEN. It could have been predicted.

MS FINANCE. I'm sorry?

ALLEN. We were warned.

JOHN. Well, threatened, actually.

ALLEN. We ignored it.

JOHN. I don't think it's helpful to –

ALLEN. What?

JOHN. Speculate.

ALLEN. No?

JOHN. Hindsight is a wonderful thing.

ALLEN. Jesus.

JOHN *turns to the others.*

JOHN. Allen is having a rough time at the moment.

ALLEN.

JOHN. I keep telling him that we're all right behind him, that we all think he's doing great things –

MR PR. He is doing great things –

MS FINANCE (*to* ALLEN). You are doing great things –

ALLEN. There's a case – (*To* JOHN.) did you tell them that? –
a lawsuit –

MR PR. We heard.

ALLEN. I'll have to testify.

JOHN. Allen –

ALLEN. I authorised it, you see.

JOHN. This isn't the time to start –

ALLEN. He wants me to take time off.

JOHN. Alright, why don't we leave it there.

ALLEN. David told me everyone makes mistakes.

> MR PR *and* MS FINANCE *stand up and turn to leave.*
> ALLEN *calls after them.*

> But David doesn't think, David doesn't have an opinion,
> because David's not a human.

JOHN. Allen –

ALLEN. And I like humans, you know?

> MR PR *and* MS FINANCE *leave.*

JOHN. What is with you?

ALLEN. Oh, can't you tell, I'm having a rough time at the
moment.

JOHN. And we are –

ALLEN. Right behind me, I know.

> ALLEN *walks out.*

> JAMIE *stares straight ahead, hands flat on top of his laptop.*

KYLA. Alright, Jamie?

> *He doesn't respond.*

> Um, yeah, so I'm staying with you for a few days.

JAMIE.

KYLA. Your dad said I could.

JAMIE.

KYLA. She OD'd. Came off the methadone too soon and then –

It happens sometimes, people think they're better and then –

Anyway, they think she'll live, so that's good.

JAMIE.

KYLA. You could say something.

JAMIE.

KYLA. Like *are you okay* or something.

JAMIE. I'm busy.

KYLA. Oh. Okay.

I'll just wait, shall I?

KYLA sits down and gets out her phone. JAMIE *opens his laptop.*

GIRLS' VOICES. Ten ways to tie your hair in a ponytail.

Nine sex positions that burn more calories than running.

Eight ways to survive a zombie apocalypse.

Seven ways to deal with girls hitting on your man.

How to achieve a bikini body in six weeks.

Five reasons other people are happier than you.

Four ways to cook an aubergine.

Three things you should know about internet privacy.

How to change your bed sheets in two minutes.

Look at this kitten –

Look at this puppy –

Look at this kitten –

Look at this puppy –

Dead cat meme: I'M NOT DEAD, I'M JUST RESTING MY EYES.

KYLA *looks up.* JAMIE *stares at his screen.*

KYLA. Did you hear about the crash?

JAMIE. Yeah.

KYLA. And?

JAMIE. And good.

KYLA. Good?

JAMIE. Yeah.

KYLA. How did they even hack something like Octopay?

He turns to KYLA.

JAMIE. It would probably have taken months. At least. They'd find an initial way into the network, like a spear-phishing email or something. Once they were in they'd start taking control of software-developer accounts and accessing source-code repositories until they got to the system's microservices. After that it'd be layers of data storage and retrieval and business logic and stuff like that until they found an exploit in the code. And then – I'm guessing – whatever malware was installed would fuck with the value system and everyone's data would be worth exactly the same: nothing.

KYLA. Oh-kaaay.

JAMIE. I'm guessing.

KYLA *thinks for a moment.*

KYLA. I don't understand why hackers are so obsessed with breaking things all the time.

JAMIE.

KYLA. Like, why can't they fix things?

JAMIE. Because sometimes the only way to fix something is to take it apart.

KYLA. Yeah, well, it's not up to Hackdolz or anyone else to decide what's wrong and what's right.

JAMIE. You don't get it.

KYLA. I do get it. I know you think I'm stupid because I'm a girl and I'm in year nine but I do actually get it and I think what they did is wrong.

JAMIE.

KYLA. Have you heard of Doctor X?

JAMIE. No.

KYLA. Doctor X helps people. There's a place you can go and he, or maybe he's a she, will give you no-strings advice so it won't bring your score down. Like me and my mum.

JAMIE. Your mum nearly died.

KYLA. That's not the point.

JAMIE. Yes, that is the point. People like Doctor X might help in the short term but they're just pushing people like you and your mum further underground. The more you're s'posed to share the more there is to hide.

KYLA. So you don't think I did the right thing, getting her the stuff?

JAMIE. It's none of my business.

KYLA. But would you do it for your mum?

JAMIE. My mum's already dead.

KYLA. But if she was alive?

JAMIE. My mum wasn't a junkie.

KYLA. No. Yeah. I know.

Why don't you talk about her?

It's good to talk you know.

JAMIE. Just stop, Kyla, just –

STOP TALKING.

JAMIE *closes his laptop and places his hands flat on top of it.*

KYLA. I used to fancy you.

JAMIE.

KYLA. But I think if we had a relationship we'd just argue all the time.

JAMIE.

KYLA. So I'm going to sleep on the sofa bed, alright?

JAMIE. Alright.

KYLA. Fine.

KYLA turns to leave.

Your dad's right. You are totally asocial.

JAMIE waits for her to leave, then opens his laptop and types a long string of letters and numbers into the address bar.

Thumping disco music and flashing lights. A HACKDOL enters. She wears a neon balaclava and long blonde Barbie-like hair. A stream of impenetrable programming language appears on various screens.

HACKDOL. This is not just a battle over the future of privacy and publicity. This is a battle for choice and informed consent.

Choose freedom. Choose autonomy. Choose independence. Choose individualism. Choose opportunity. Choose to educate yourself. Choose to open your eyes. Choose to use your voice.

We all have a right to this space. We all have a duty to hold on to it. Together we have the power to say NO to the governments who spy on us in the name of security, NO to the corporations who steal from us in the name of convenience and NO to the media who profit from our ignorance.

Enough is enough.

If you are a human being who believes in the freedom of information, join us.

And remember this: those who surrender freedom –

Suddenly lights up on JAMIE at his laptop. The HACKDOL freezes. She and JAMIE stare at one another throughout.

Two POLICEMEN *enter, followed by* STEVE.

POLICEMAN #1. Jamie Smith?

STEVE. Officer, there's been a misunderstanding.

POLICEMAN #2 *handcuffs* JAMIE.

POLICEMAN #1. You are under arrest for computer hacking, computer fraud, obstruction of justice and conspiracy to access multiple networks without authorisation. You do not have to say anything but it may harm your defence if you do not mention when questioned something which you later rely on in court. Anything you say may be given in evidence.

KYLA *enters*.

KYLA. Jamie?

STEVE (*to* POLICEMEN). Now hold on, you can't just –

POLICEMAN #1 *picks up* JAMIE*'s laptop and searches the room for other devices*.

(*To* KYLA.) Did you know about this?

KYLA *shakes her head*.

(*To* POLICEMEN.) Officers, there has clearly been a terrible misunderstanding. I know it took a while but he apologised to Mr Mosedale about the penis –

POLICEMAN #1 (*to* POLICEMAN #2). All clear.

STEVE. Innocent until proven guilty.

POLICEMAN #1. 'Scuse me, sir.

The POLICEMEN *lead* JAMIE *out.* KYLA *blocks their path.*

Out the way, miss.

KYLA. Can't I at least say goodbye?

They stop for a moment. KYLA *goes to* JAMIE.

Goodbye, Jamie.

JAMIE.

KYLA. I'm sorry I said that thing about arguing.

JAMIE.

KYLA. I like arguing with you.

JAMIE.

KYLA. I think actually if we had a relationship we'd argue really well together, I think –

POLICEMAN #1. Alright, that's enough.

> *The* POLICEMEN *lead him out and* KYLA *and* STEVE *are left alone.*

KYLA. I'm looking after it. The other laptop.

> STEVE *nods but can't respond.*

> So, um, are you ready for the best spaghetti hoops you've ever tasted?

> *The sound of handcuffs clicking on and off. A cell door slamming shut. The world spins on its axis. Lights flicker on and off – faulty strip lighting or night turning day. A digital clock speeds up, turning months to weeks to days until –*

> *Two court cases occurring simultaneously over days, weeks, months. A* JUDGE *switches their attention between the two. Their hammer hits the table.*

PROSECUTOR #1. Your Honour, counsel, ladies and gentlemen of the jury, this is a clear case of the misuse of private information and breach of confidence.

PROSECUTOR #2. Do not be fooled by his age. Do not be fooled by his mild manner. The boy you see before you is a danger to the safety and security of you and your family.

PROSECUTOR #1. The evidence will show that not only did Octopus Inc. acquire data that was *illegally* procured by a convicted cybercriminal, but that they have profited and will continue to profit from it.

PROSECUTOR #2. The defence will argue that Jamie Smith was a follower, that he fell in with the wrong crowd. But the evidence will show that Jamie Smith in fact *masterminded* this attack from his bedroom in South London.

LAWYER #1. Your Honour, counsel, ladies and gentlemen of the jury, if you saw a starving kitten in the street, would you leave it there not knowing who might find it or what they might do with it, or would you take it home and feed it?

LAWYER #2. Did you ever do something stupid when you were sixteen? Did you, say, steal a chocolate bar from your local shop? Jump the barriers at a Tube station?

LAWYER #1. And imagine you had taken that poor starving kitten home, and imagine you'd looked after it, given it something to eat – would you then think it okay for the previous owners to sue you for billions of dollars?

LAWYER #2. My Lord, this is a boy who did something stupid. He just happened to do that something stupid on the internet.

LAWYER #1. It's not illegal to take what's already public. When information is made available on the World Wide Web, however it might be procured, that information is effectively published to the world.

LAWYER #2. The evidence will show that my client was one small cog in a much bigger machine. There is no way that this sixteen-year-old boy, sitting in his bedroom in South London, could have foreseen the consequences of his actions.

ALLEN*'s signature flashes up on various screens.*

PROSECUTOR #1. Your Honour, I would like to refer to exhibit forty-two, the instruction submitted by Allen Young when he authorised the collection of my clients' data *after* it was published by Gary White, aka Houdini.

Screen-grabs from anonymous chat rooms flash up on various screens.

PROSECUTOR #2. Please pay attention to exhibit fifty-one in which the accused writes, quote, *cocksuckers got what was coming to them*, unquote.

PROSECUTOR #1. The plaintiffs call Allen Young to the stand.

CLERK (*to* ALLEN). Do you swear that the testimony you are about to give is the truth, the whole truth and nothing but the truth?

PROSECUTOR #2. The prosecution calls Mr Nigel Mosedale to the stand.

CLERK (*to* MR MOSEDALE). Do you swear that the testimony you are about to give is the truth, the whole truth and nothing but the truth?

PROSECUTOR #1. Please state your full name.

ALLEN. Allen Young.

PROSECUTOR #1. How long have you worked at Octopus Inc., Mr Young?

ALLEN. Nine years.

PROSECUTOR #1. And during those nine years the company has gone from being a smallish start-up to a global corporation with an annual revenue exceeding sixteen billion dollars, has it not?

ALLEN. I believe it's something like that.

PROSECUTOR #1. And is it fair to say that as a partner you had a vested interest in, let's say, *growing* the company?

ALLEN. Well of course.

PROSECTOR #1. And is it fair to say that occasionally you might have cut corners to, let's say, *speed up* the process?

LAWYER #1. Objection. Relevance.

PROSECUTOR #2. Please state your full name.

MR MOSEDALE. Nigel Mosedale.

PROSECUTOR #2. Do you know the defendant, Mr Mosedale?

MR MOSEDALE. Yes I do.

PROSECUTOR #2. What is your relationship to the defendant?

MR MOSEDALE. I am a headmaster and Jamie Smith attends – attended – my school.

PROSECUTOR #2. How many students attend your school, Mr Mosedale?

MR MOSEDALE. Two thousand, give or take.

PROSECUTOR #2. It must be hard to remember the names and faces of some two thousand students.

MR MOSEDALE. I try, but yes, it is hard.

PROSECUTOR #2. But the name Jamie Smith rang a bell for you, did it not?

MR MOSEDALE. It did.

PROSECUTOR #2. Why is that?

MR MOSEDALE. Because last year Jamie Smith hacked into the network and –

PROSECUTOR #2. Go on.

MR MOSEDALE. And posted a photograph of a penis on the school homepage.

LAWYER #2. Objection. Ruled inadmissible.

GARY*'s signature flashes up on various screens.*

PROSECUTOR #1. Your Honour, I would like to refer to exhibit eighty-four, the contract signed by convicted cybercriminal Gary White, aka Houdini, the day Allen Young *offered him a job* at Octopus Inc.

Screen-grabs of numbers and locations flash up on various screens.

PROSECUTOR #2. Please pay attention as best you can to exhibit ninety-three, in particular the IP address used to log in to the VPN server at the time the defendant was arrested at his home in South London.

LAWYER #1. Mr Young, did you ever *deny* offering Gary White a job at Octopus Inc.?

ALLEN. No I did not.

LAWYER #1. And did you ever *deny* authorising the use of public data?

ALLEN. No I did not.

LAWYER #1. Could you explain your reasoning behind your *not denying* these facts to the court?

ALLEN. Because I wasn't doing anything wrong. I wasn't doing anything illegal.

LAWYER #1. No further questions.

LAWYER #2. My Lord, the fact that my client posted an inappropriate image on his school's homepage has no bearing on his role in the attack on Octopus Inc. If anything, the photograph of the penis undermines the prosecution's argument. This is a boy who wants to make his friends laugh. This is not a boy who cares about the ins and outs of data-market algorithms.

LAWYER #1. Your Honour, I return to the question of the starving kitten –

LAWYER #2. The defence calls the defendant Jamie Smith to the stand.

LAWYER #1. If you were to take the kitten home and kill it that would be one thing, but Mr Young did not kill the kitten.

CLERK (*to* JAMIE). Do you swear that the testimony you are about to give is the truth, the whole truth and nothing but the truth?

LAWYER #1. First of all, there was no code-based restriction preventing Mr Young from accessing and using that data and at no point did Octopus Inc. misuse the data they collected. Secondly, the fact that Mr Young visited Gary White some six months ago has nothing to do with Mr Young's authorising the use of that data and has no bearing on the charges brought against my client.

LAWYER #2. Please state your full name.

JAMIE. Jamie Smith.

LAWYER #2. How old are you, Jamie?

JAMIE. Sixteen.

LAWYER #2. Sixteen. And did you, at the start of year eleven, post a photograph of a penis on your school's homepage?

JAMIE. Yes.

LAWYER #2. Can you explain to the court what was going through your mind when you posted that image?

JAMIE.

LAWYER #2. Did you think it was funny, for example?

JAMIE. No.

LAWYER #2. You didn't think it was funny.

PROSECUTOR #2. Objection.

JAMIE. No.

LAWYER #2. You didn't think a naked penis on a school website was funny.

PROSECUTOR #2. Leading question.

JAMIE. No.

It was a protest.

LAWYER #2. A protest, right, a student protest.

JAMIE.

LAWYER #2. And did this protest have anything to do with the Hackdolz?

JAMIE. Hackdolz.

LAWYER #2.

JAMIE. There's no *the*.

LAWYER #2.

JAMIE. And no. That was nothing to do with Hackdolz.

LAWYER #2. For the benefit of the jury could you clarify who or what Hackdolz is.

JAMIE. It's an anonymous hacking group.

LAWYER #2. And are you in any way associated with this group?

JAMIE. Yeah.

LAWYER #2. In what capacity?

JAMIE. We talk online.

We share code and stuff.

LAWYER #2. And roughly how many members belong to this group?

JAMIE. Dunno.

LAWYER #2. But it's a lot, is it?

JAMIE. Probably, yeah.

LAWYER #2. And when you were communicating with this group, *Hackdolz*, did you at any point realise that they were planning a cyber attack on Octopus Inc.?

LAWYER #2 *shoots him a meaningful look.*

JAMIE. Yeah.

LAWYER #2. Let me rephrase that –

JAMIE. It was my idea.

LAWYER #2 *frowns at him.*

LAWYER #2. But you didn't realise – I mean, how could you realise – that attack would cause the entire data market to crash.

JAMIE. No, yeah, I did.

LAWYER #2 *opens and closes their mouth a few times.*

LAWYER #2. Then can you explain to the court, and me, what was going through your mind when you came to this realisation?

JAMIE.

LAWYER #2. Did you think it was funny, for example?

JAMIE. No.

LAWYER #2. Another protest?

JAMIE. Not a protest. A battle.

LAWYER #2 *sighs.*

LAWYER #2. No further questions.

PROSECUTOR #1. Ladies and gentlemen of the jury, you have heard for yourselves how Octopus Inc. acquired data that was *illegally* procured –

PROSECUTOR #2. The prosecution have proved beyond reasonable doubt that Jamie Smith is guilty –

PROSECUTOR #1. Is it fair that Octopus Inc. continue to profit from *stolen* data?

PROSECUTOR #2. By his own admission, the defendant is a highly skilled black-hat hacker who not only was involved with the group Hackdolz but indeed *masterminded* the attack on Octopus –

LAWYER #1. Ladies and gentlemen of the jury, I ask you this: what kind of a world do you want to live in? A world that is open, accessible, transparent –

LAWYER #2. My client believes in a world in which citizens have the right to choose what and how they share –

LAWYER #1. Or a world in which criminals have free reign to wreak havoc on the lives of innocent people –

LAWYER #2. He is prepared to sacrifice his own freedom for the freedom of others –

LAWYER #1. Innocent people and starving kittens –

LAWYER #2. But ladies and gentlemen of the jury, I ask you to think back to when *you* were sixteen, and ask yourself how *you* would feel if that one stupid mistake had cost you your freedom.

The JUDGE*'s hammer hits the table. The courtrooms disperse.*

A prison visiting room. KYLA *and* GARY *sit across from one another at a table.*

KYLA. Alright, Dad?

GARY. Kyla.

KYLA.

GARY. You're so big.

KYLA. I'm fifteen.

GARY. I know.

KYLA.

GARY.

KYLA.

GARY. How's Stacey?

KYLA. Good. Yeah. Clean.

GARY. Good.

KYLA.

GARY. Kyla, I'm sorry –

KYLA. For what.

GARY. For everything.

    KYLA *shrugs*.

KYLA. You were busy.

GARY. It's not an excuse.

KYLA. Busy being someone else.

GARY.

KYLA.

GARY. Did she ever –

    Stacey, did she ever –

KYLA. Mum never talked about you.

GARY.

KYLA. I was curious.

GARY. Curious.

KYLA. Why did you name your virus after me?

    GARY *thinks, then looks at her.*

GARY. 'Cause it's beautiful and powerful and it fucks with the establishment.

KYLA. Yeah but –

GARY.

KYLA. You don't know me.

GARY. Yeah. Well. I want to.

KYLA.

GARY.

KYLA. Did you hear about Hackdolz?

GARY. Course.

KYLA. He's my friend. Jamie Smith.

GARY. Yeah?

KYLA. Used to go to my school.

GARY. Nice lad?

KYLA. Helped me buy methadone.

GARY. What?

KYLA. I'm looking after his other laptop.

GARY. Kyla, be careful.

KYLA. I am being careful.

I deleted MyCloud.

GARY.

KYLA. That's a pretty radical thing to do at my age.

GARY. No, I get it.

KYLA. I'm thinking about adopting a cat.

I think I'm good at looking after things.

People. Laptops. Cats.

I think I'm good at fixing things.

GARY. Yeah?

KYLA. Yeah. I think actually I'm quite different to the virus you named after me.

GARY.

KYLA.

GARY. Yeah. I think you're right.

> *An apartment in Bucharest.* CANDY, *now* NATALIA, *opens a door. She wears civilian clothes, no wig and less make-up.*

NATALIA. Allen?

ALLEN. Candy.

NATALIA. What are you doing here?

ALLEN. I tried to find you –

NATALIA. I leave studio.

ALLEN. I know, I looked you up –

NATALIA. Why are you come to Romania?

ALLEN. Because I have something for you.

> *A Georges Seurat painting of the sea flashes up on various screens, some showing it in its entirety, some zooming in on the dots of colour.*

NATALIA. For me?

ALLEN. You said you liked paintings.

NATALIA.

ALLEN. And I thought –

> I don't know what I thought.

> I just wanted to see you.

> In person.

> NATALIA *stares at the painting.*

NATALIA. I can't.

ALLEN. No, it's a present, for you.

NATALIA. I can't take it.

ALLEN. Why not?

NATALIA. Because it remind me of –

ALLEN. What?

NATALIA. Sorry, my English is not –

ALLEN. Candy?

NATALIA. Natalia. My name is Natalia.

ALLEN. Right.

NATALIA.

ALLEN.

NATALIA. I try make new life after –

I try forget –

ALLEN. I know it must've been hard when –

I know what it feels like to be in the public eye.

NATALIA. Yes?

ALLEN. And I know what it's like to be publicly humiliated.

NATALIA. You also have people say they rape and kill you?

ALLEN. Well, no, but –

NATALIA.

ALLEN.

NATALIA. Candy is old life.

ALLEN. I told you things. I told you things I never told anyone.

NATALIA. It was my job.

ALLEN. No. Your job was to take your clothes off and I never asked you to take your clothes off.

NATALIA. I'm sorry, Allen. I like you but –

Candy isn't real.

ALLEN. But this. This is real. Me. Standing here.

This is as real as it gets.

Isn't it?

A promotional video plays. Shards of crystal catch the light. Simple visuals illustrate the message.

VOICE-OVER. Be in control of your data.

Be in control of your life.

When you share data with Crystal, we share our algorithms with you, so you know exactly how to build up your score.

Open your eyes. Use your voice. Be part of a community that values choice and informed consent.

Enter a new era of sharing that is totally open, totally equal and always transparent.

Cut the mystery, cut the jargon, get straight to Crystal.

Shards of crystal shimmer, then disappear.

A prison visiting room. JAMIE *and* RACHEL *sit across from one another at a table.*

JAMIE. I'm not interested.

RACHEL. Just hear me out.

JAMIE. You want me to work for Crystal.

RACHEL. Not for. With.

JAMIE. Well I'm not interested.

RACHEL. Jamie, you're seventeen years old.

JAMIE. I know.

RACHEL. Your talent is wasted in here.

JAMIE. I know.

RACHEL. So do something with it.

JAMIE. I will.

RACHEL. There's a good chance our lawyers could get you early release.

JAMIE. That's exactly what Allen Young said to Gary White.

RACHEL. Yes, well, Gary White broke his contract and his word.

JAMIE. Funny how when a hacker gets caught they're locked up for hundreds of years but when a corporation gets caught it's a fine and a slap on the wrist.

RACHEL. Octopus paid out a billion dollars in damages. I'd call that more than a slap on the wrist.

JAMIE. Octopus, Crystal – they're all the same.

RACHEL. Actually our ethos is very different.

This is a new era of sharing. Totally open, totally equal –

JAMIE. Always transparent, I know.

RACHEL. I'm not asking you to go against everything you believe in. I'm asking you to help us build something beautiful.

The internet is not black and white, Jamie. It's not a case of you versus us. We're actually, relatively speaking, on the same page. We want to empower our users with choice and information.

With minds like yours, who knows what we could achieve.

A long pause.

I fly back this evening. Think about it.

RACHEL *gets up*. JAMIE *watches her leave*.

Blackout.

End.

Other Titles in this Series

A Nick Hern Book

Darknet first published in Great Britain as a paperback original in 2016 by Nick Hern Books Limited, The Glasshouse, 49a Goldhawk Road, London W12 8QP, in association with Potential Difference and Southwark Playhouse, London

Darknet copyright © 2016 Rose Lewenstein

Rose Lewenstein has asserted her right to be identified as the author of this work

Cover image: Rebecca Pitt

Designed and typeset by Nick Hern Books, London
Printed in the UK by Mimeo Ltd, Huntingdon, Cambridgeshire PE29 6XX

A CIP catalogue record for this book is available from the British Library

ISBN 978 1 84842 581 1

Woodland
CARBON
www.woodlandcarbon.co.uk
NICK HERN BOOKS
Printed on Carbon Captured paper

www.nickhernbooks.co.uk

facebook.com/nickhernbooks

twitter.com/nickhernbooks